Note: In this book common plant names are given first, followed by their botanical names in italics. The botanical names are in many cases more precise. For example, the entry **Barberry** (*Berberis thunbergii*) (p112) applies to a specific barberry recommended for its autumn colour; there are other barberries that would be less suitable. When buying plants listed in this book, ensure that botanical names tally.

The Mitchell Beazley Pocket Guide to Gardening
First published in Great Britain in 1987 by Mitchell Beazley Publishers

Copyright ©1987 Mitchell Beazley Publishers

This edition published in 1995 by Mitchell Beazley,
an imprint of Reed Consumer Books Limited,
Michelin House, 81 Fulham Road, London, SW3 6RB, and Auckland,
Melbourne, Singapore and Toronto.

ISBN 1 85732 579 6

A CIP catalogue record for this book is available from the British Library.

Designed and produced by The Bridgewater Book Company Limited
Printed and bound in France by Imprimerie Pollina SA

CONTENTS

This book is a hint-giver and memory-jogger. All gardeners worth their growmore will already have one or more of the bulkier books on gardening, but exhaustive coverage can be frustrating when all you need is a shortlist of a dozen or so plants to fill a sunny pocket on a rock garden or a concise account of pruning methods for clematis. *The Pocket Guide to Gardening* concentrates on fundamentals. Its list-by-list organization is a practical way to present both planting recommendations – what to grow where – and hundreds of how-to tips on garden structure, tools and techniques. The pocket format means that you can take this book where it will be most useful – to the garden centre, the garden or the greenhouse. It will easily fit in your jacket pocket or trug basket.

There are thousands of keen gardeners in Britain and hundreds of thousands of others who enjoy sitting or strolling in a garden but are baffled by the apparent mystery surrounding this ancient craft – and by the barrage of Latin names and bewildering range of species and varieties. That's sad. In reality, gardening is fifty per cent common sense, twenty-five per cent know-how, twenty per cent perspiration and five per cent luck. This book can't offer much in the way of muscle power, but it does offer the common sense and know-how. With *The Pocket Guide to Gardening* in your possession, you're seventy-five per cent a gardener. All you need now are barrowloads of energy and a pinch of luck!

GARDEN STRUCTURE AND DESIGN

BASIC OPTIONS

When planning a garden, first analyse the potential offered by the site. Then go on to consider the style you want to create, the budget available and the time you are able or willing to spend on maintenance.

■ Three factors in garden planning

Every garden has its own microclimate, determined by local factors, including soil, aspect and structure. The slope of the land influences the amount of sunlight received, in turn affecting the length of the growing season. Clay soils warm up more slowly than sandy soils – but retain the heat longer. Walls of stone or brick absorb and emit heat, so that you can grow more tender plants against them. The ground at the leeward side of the wall or a line of trees will be sheltered from rain, and may need frequent watering. Altitude is also a factor: the higher, the colder. Dense urban surroundings, on the other hand, have a warming effect.

• **Aspect** Ensure that greenhouses, flower borders, vegetable and fruit plots, patios and pools receive good light. Put compost heaps, sheds and beds for ferns and other shade-loving plants where light intensity is low. Remember that trees and buildings cast longer midday shadows in winter.

• **Topography** Avoid placing fruit trees and other frost-sensitive plants in dips or hollows, where cold air may collect at night. Plots exposed to high winds should be equipped with windbreaks. In coastal regions, where the wind may be laden with salt, special care is needed over plant selection. Where the angle of slope makes gardening difficult, consider building terraces to solve the problem.

• **Soil** Garden with the soil, not against it. Do not attempt to grow lime-hating plants on alkaline soil, lime-lovers in acid peat, or moisture-lovers in sharp-draining sand.

■ Five visual aspects of garden design

If possible you should plan the garden to present a series of changing views as you walk around it. Remember to take the view from the house windows into account.

• **Relationship of house and garden** Soften the area between the two with a patio, or by growing climbers against the house, or plants in hanging baskets or window boxes.

• **Trees** If you have established trees, plan the garden design around them. Plant new trees where they will not obscure good views onto neighbours' gardens.

• **Paving and paths** Sometimes known as the "hardscape" of the garden. Use materials that blend well with the house. Plan paths to give convenient speedy access to vegetables, herbs and the greenhouse in bad weather.

• **Lines** Curves are usually more pleasing than straight edges, unless you want a deliberately formal garden. Make bold curves, not fussy ones. When planning beds and lawn shapes, take ease of mowing into account.

• **Outbuildings** Utility buildings – the shed and the greenhouse – should be screened off in a separate area of the garden if possible. Ugly walls of sheds or garages may be disguised by a creeper-clad trellis or a line of shrubs.

■ Three aspects of planting choice

Make a shortlist of the plants that will suit your particular site. Then base your final choice on shape, texture and colour, as well as maintenance requirements. When designing a shrub or mixed border, draw up a plan on paper and number the plants according to the months they will be at their best, to help to plan a good year-round display.

• **Texture and form** Contrast delicate foliage with large bold leaves, and use upright plants as a foil for those of spreading habit. Group smaller plants so that their impact is not lost, and make sure they will not be hidden by larger plants.

• **Colour** Many people find that a mixture of vivid colours jostling one another is less pleasing than subtle contrasts or harmonies. Plan flowering in groups, so that one group of plants is coming into bloom as another group is fading. Fiery reds, oranges and yellows planted in small patches will have as much impact as larger masses of blues and greens. A single-colour garden (white is especially popular) will benefit from a foliage framework in various shades of green and grey.

• **Scent** Place richly scented plants near the windows of the house or along paths, where you can enjoy maximum benefit. Consider using scented carpet plants (such as thyme or chamomile) in paving areas.

■ Seven hints for a labour-saving garden

Elderly gardeners or those with limited leisure time can avoid many routine tasks (such as weeding and mowing) by careful planning and plant selection.

• **Avoid labour-intensive plants** – that is, those that require a lot of pruning, staking and dead heading. Many shrubs are very easy to manage.

• **Eradicate weeds** by groundcover planting, mulching and discriminating use of weedkillers.

• **Make hard surfaces** to reduce the area of lawn. Gravel, paving and concrete need no more than a rake or broom to keep them tidy.

• **Create long-grass areas** in the lawn, with mown grass confined to circulation areas. Daffodils and other bulbs can be planted in the long grass for seasonal colour.

• **Grow informal hedges,** not formal ones, to cut down on pruning and maintenance.

• **Make raised beds** to avoid bending. Build from brick, stone or thick wooden planks. Place a 23cm/9in layer of rubble in the bottom, then a layer of old sods, grass side down, then fill with good garden soil.

• **Confine roses** to old-fashioned shrub roses, which need little pruning.

■ Six ways to make a small garden seem larger

Part of the secret is to contrive tantalizing glimpses, suggesting there is more to the garden than meets the eye.

• **Open fencing,** such as picket fencing or trelliswork, will extend the view beyond the garden.

• **Shrubs** grown around the edges of the garden will disguise walls and solid fences to create a softened outline and reduce the sense of confinement.

• **Dividing the garden** into compartments, using trellis screens or lines of shrubs or trees, will disguise the scale of the plot. This makes the area seem larger.

• **False perspective effects** can increase the sense of distance. For example, a lawn might be made to taper towards the end. Or you could arrange trees or shrubs in diminishing heights. You can give apparent depth to a wall by placing a panel of trellis against it, with the battens pointing inwards towards an imaginary vanishing point.

• **Bands of light and shadow** created by flanking lines of trees will seem to broaden the plot.

• **Large mirrors** are sometimes used in small patio gardens to reflect plants and paving.

■ Five ornamental features

Statuary, urns, bird baths, gate finials, obelisks and other ornaments are widely available in reconstituted stone.

• **Maze** Traditionally, small-scale mazes are of fragrant plants like hyssop, santolina or thyme. Turf mazes are also popular – after cutting the paths, fill in with gravel. You could also use brick, chosen to match the brickwork of the house.

• **Topiary** Yew and box are the most popular plants. Keep shapes simple – pyramids are particularly effective.

• **Staddle stone** Mushroom-shaped construction, about 60cm/2ft high. Originally used as supports for a grain store, preventing invasion by rats. Appropriate in cottage gardens.

• **Sundial** Traditionally supported on a stone baluster, often fluted. Wall sundials are a space-saving alternative. Both available in modern reproductions.

• **Beehives** Attractive when painted white.

WALLS

Of the vertical elements in a garden, walls are probably the most effective, yet the most expensive. The mellow tones of brick or stone harmonize with plants and lawn.

■ Two basic types of wall

Excluded from consideration here are load-bearing types, which are usually architect-designed.

• **Freestanding** Freestanding walls not only define boundaries but also maintain a degree of privacy, limit invasion by neighbouring animals, protect against cold winds and act as hosts to climbing plants.

• **Retaining** These walls hold back earth – or water if they are used as pool surrounds. They must be very strong to resist the sideways pressure. Retaining walls sometimes slope back from the perpendicular, creating a "batter": this lowers the centre of gravity, making the wall more stable.

■ Eight factors that affect a wall's stability

Foundations must be deep enough to carry the wall, so that it is unaffected by movements in underlying and surrounding soil. Normally, foundations are of strong concrete.

Sand, gravel and cement for making mortar must be really clean – as must the water for mixing. Mortar is best made to set slightly weaker than the material of which the wall is made. Any slight movement and subsequent cracking will then take place in the joint, where it is more easily repaired.

• **Foundation width** As a general rule, the foundation width of a freestanding wall should be twice the upper thickness. Retaining walls, however, often have an extra wide foundation – up to as much as a third more. This additional width (known as a "toe") is on the soil side of the foundation. The soil bearing down upon it prevents the possibility of tipping.

• **Foundation depth** Depends on how supportive the soil is. Flexible clays or sands require the deepest foundations, as they are the most unstable. Undisturbed stone, or hard chalky soil, needs the least depth. For walls up to, say, 90cm/3ft high a foundation depth equivalent to one third of the wall's height should be adequate. For walls that are to be above this height, it is advisable to seek professional advice on the nature of the subsoil in your area.

• **Wall thickness** For stability and strength, thickness must be related to height. A retaining wall should generally be thicker than a freestanding wall of the same vertical dimensions. A low retaining wall, up to 30cm/12in, needs a thickness of at least 23cm/9in. Up to 90cm/3ft, allow at least 30cm/12in. Above 90cm/3ft, seek professional advice. A freestanding wall might be 11.25cm/4½in thick up to 60cm/2ft high. Above that, make the thickness at least 23cm/9in. Seek professional advice and check at what height you need to obtain permission. Approval is usually necessary for any wall constructed next to a public footpath or a public place, for example. (This is a broad gener-alization: check the rules for your own area.)

• **Piers** Sometimes included in a wall for even greater strength. Usually each side of the square is twice the wall thickness. The normal spacing is 2–3 times the wall height.

• **Damp-proofing** To prevent damage and staining, freestand-ing walls must be protected from rising damp. The usual method is to include a bituminous, or plastic, DPC (damp-proof course). Unfortunately, this is not always practicable. Such a DPC would physically separate the bottom section of the wall from the top, with the result that any undue pressure from the sides might tip the wall over. To prevent this, incor-porate a DPC consisting of several courses of a strong impervi-ous brick bonded with an equally impervious mortar at the base of the wall. You can then build the main body of the wall in a different brick, or alternatively in a different type of material altogether.

• **Capping or coping** To prevent water penetration from above, you could use a similar brick to that used at the bot-tom. Alternatively, special coping stones are obtainable in vari-ous shapes and sizes.

• **Protection from sideways damp** Necessary for retaining walls. Coat the rear side of the wall with a bituminous paint (this is known as "tanking"), or fix sheets of heavy-duty poly-thene against the back. Then put clean gravel or other drainage material in place before backfilling with soil. "Weep holes" are normally left at the base of retaining walls: water runs through these, preventing the build-up of pressure.

• **Length of wall** For a long wall, vertical thermal movement joints are recommended. Without these joints the wall will either expand and bulge or shrink and crack.

■ Four materials for walls

Use local materials if possible. Try to ensure that the wall is aesthetically compatible with the house.

• **Brick** Thousands of brick types available, but not all are suitable for retaining walls: always check with a builder or with the relevant brick association. If possible, choose a brick that will harmonize with existing brickwork. In certain areas you have to obtain planning permission for both brick colour and texture. For all exterior work, bricks should generally be durable and frost-proof. The standard size is 22x10x6.5cm/ 8⅝x4x2⅝in, allowing for a 1cm/⅜in mortared joint. Other sizes are available for various specialized uses.

• **Natural stone** Should also be strong and durable, and preferably not newly quarried as many stones only look attractive when weathered. If using stratified stones, lay the striations horizontally to prevent water penetration. Stone walls may be built of random stone paves (rubble) or of dressed stone. Drystone walls (built without mortar) call for a great deal of skill, but have certain advantages. They are "flexible" and take any slight movements into themselves without damage. They are usually self-draining and require no concrete foundation – just a series of very large stones laid in a trench at their bottom. Drystone walls are normally much thicker than mortar-bonded walls and need "bonding" stones or "through" stones to key the outer faces together.

• **Concrete** Most concrete blocks for gardens use imitation natural stone. The bonds are the same as for natural stone. Some manufacturers issue special building instructions and bonding patterns. Concrete blocks must be durable and frost-proof. Available in many colours, finishes, sizes and textures. Concrete pierced screen units are also available. These are usually square, in grey or white. They are normally "stack-bonded": follow supplier's instructions.

• **Timber** Stout logs or planks driven into the ground side by side to half their length, make attractive retaining walls, especially for raised alpines and dwarf conifer beds. Treat logs with a preservative.

FENCES

Fences are constructed *in situ* or from pre-fabricated units or sections. There is a broad repertoire of materials, including timber (sawn, split or slatted), wire, plastic, metal bars or concrete, each of which has its own distinct character.

■ Six types of open fence

An "open" fence affords views beyond, preventing a claustrophobic effect in a small garden. Such fences, while reducing wind speed, are also less likely to be blown over by wind and they offer a framework for planting. Against this you need to balance the need for privacy.

• **Post and rail** Mostly seen in the countryside. Stout oak or chestnut posts are driven well into the ground, and 2 or 3 horizontal bars (split boughs, trunks or roughly sawn timber) are attached by nailing or mortice-jointing. Wire mesh is sometimes attached to the back to make the fence stock-proof, with a strand of barbed wire along the top; however, the latter would not be permitted in a town.

• **Picket or palisade** Stout supporting posts driven into the ground carry horizontal "arris" rails to which are attached vertical palisades or pickets, spaced at close intervals. The tops may be shaped decoratively. If oak, the fence can be left untreated; otherwise treat it with preservative or paint it (preferably white).

• **Chestnut paling** A useful temporary or semi-permanent fence, simply made from split chestnut branches of uniform length, spaced, and bound vertically with galvanized wire. Sold in rolls of various lengths and heights. Must be stretched and fixed to spaced stout sawn or rounded posts that are driven well into the ground. End-posts usually need angled overarm support to keep them upright.

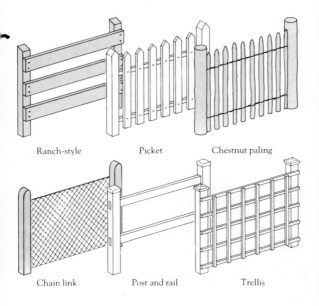

Ranch-style   Picket   Chestnut paling

Chain link   Post and rail   Trellis

• **Chain link** Formed of "knitted wire", either galvanized or covered in plastic. Not attractive on its own, but makes a good support for climbing plants. Black or olive green is best colour choice, blending into the shadows of surrounding plants, shrubs and trees. Avoid the bright, almost fluorescent, green sometimes seen. Quality of both wire and accompanying purpose-made angle-iron straining and intermediate posts varies greatly. Success of fence will depend on tautness of horizontal supporting wires to which chain links is attached, usually with hog rings. Where rabbits are a problem, chain link may be set well down into the earth, to prevent burrowing under.

• **Ranch-style fence** Horizontal boards (usually 2 or 3) spaced at regular intervals and secured to posts. Usually white-painted.

• **Trellis** Square or diamond pattern. Can be used on its own, supported by posts, or placed on top of solid fencing to soften the line. Looks best with climbing plants. Folding trellis must be set into a rigid frame.

■ Three types of solid fence

Some solid fences act as a sail and may blow over in a high wind. If the site is exposed, choose an open fence (above).

• **Interwoven or overlap** Normally mass-produced in panels 1.8m/6ft wide. Heights vary from 60cm/2ft to 1.8m/6ft. Thin slats of wood are interwoven or overlapped, supported by vertical battens, and the whole framed and capped. Larch is commonly used timber. Panels must be supported by good strong posts approximately 8cm/3in square, set well into the ground and concreted in at the bottom, or secured in special supports that are first driven into the ground. Both posts and panels are treated with a brown preservative which should be non-toxic to plants. Sometimes concrete posts are used instead of timber. Interwoven or overlap fences step down with changes in level, so allow for this when ordering post lengths.

• **Close board** More expensive, but also more durable. Usually erected *in situ*. Strong supporting posts concreted into the

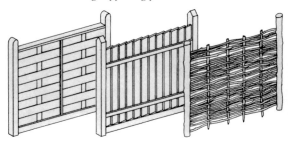

Interwoven   Close board   Wattle hurdle

ground carry 2 or 3 horizontal arris rails. To these are
attached, by nailing, either butt-jointed horizontal boards
approximately 1–1.25cm/⅜–½in thick, or feathered partially
overlapping boards of a similar thickness. A timber capping
keeps the weather from the end grain, while at the bottom is
a horizontal gravel board which you can replace easily and
inexpensively when deterioration begins.

• **Wattle hurdle** Excellent for instant fence-making, and a
good foil for climbers or other plants. Wattle hurdles – originally mobile enclosures for sheep farming – are still made
today in some areas by basket-weaving flexible willow or
chestnut branches into a rectangle. Each hurdle may embody
a series of sharpened stakes which can be driven into the
ground. However, panels can equally well be attached to an
existing wire fence.

HEDGES

**Unlike some walls or fences, hedges improve with
age – provided that they are well looked after. They
form a soft and natural background while filtering
the wind to create a warmer micro-climate. When
choosing the hedging plants, consider aspect and soil
first, then appearance. In exposed conditions the
plants should be very hardy, perhaps using indige-
nous species. Choose good strong bushy plants, not
tall leggy ones. Good site preparation is essential, as
the hedge is likely to be in place for many years.
Prepare a trench or strip incorporating plenty of
humus and a slow-release fertilizer. Conifers should
always be planted as a single row. Some hedges, such
as beech or thorn, may be planted as two staggered
rows to ensure a good impenetrable boundary.**

■ Two aspects of hedge maintenance

Like any other plants, hedges need watering and the
occasional feed. Mulching is of benefit in the early years.

• **Shape and size** In cross-section a hedge should be wider at
the bottom than at the top. This allows as much light as possible to fall on the sides. If the lower part is in the shadow of
the top, weak basal growth will result. Only allow the hedge
to grow to the height appropriate for its function, remember-
ing that large areas of shade it may cast will make it difficult
to cultivate other plants.

• **Clipping** Formal hedges should be clipped regularly to
keep them neat and maintain dense growth. If growth gets
out of hand and you have to give a drastic cut, you may spoil
the shape of the hedge or even kill it (especially if it is conif-
erous). Optimum time of year for clipping varies according to
the plant. Hedges with exceptionally large leaves, such as

laurel, must be pruned, not clipped. Informal hedges are left to grow naturally; most are valued for their flowers or berries.

■ Seven formal broad-leaved hedges

These popular hedging plants with large or medium-sized leaves include both evergreens and deciduous types. The leaves are generally oval in shape.

• **Beech** (*Fagus sylvatica*) Popular deciduous hedging plant with large oval leaves which start off bright green in spring. The dead leaves, in a lovely shade of golden-brown, are held throughout the winter. Grows well on chalky soils and tolerates exposed windy sites. Plant 45cm/18in apart and clip once a year, in late summer. Quite a fast grower.

• **Firethorn** (*Pyracantha rogersiana*) Evergreen shrub with narrow, oval, deep-green leaves and very spiny stems, ideal for an impenetrable hedge. If not trimmed too hard, will produce orange-red berries in autumn. For a good crop of berries grow as semi-formal hedge, clipping only lightly. Very tough – grows anywhere. Plant 30cm/12in apart and trim in spring or early summer. A fast grower.

• **Hawthorn** (*Crataegus monogyna*) Deciduous shrub with extremely spiny stems and medium green lobed leaves. If not trimmed too hard, will produce white flowers in spring followed by red berries. Fast grower, especially recommended for coastal and exposed windy gardens; excellent on clay soils. Plant 30cm/12in apart; for a very formal hedge, trim once a month from late spring to late summer.

• **Holly** (*Ilex aquifolium*) Slow-growing evergreen with very prickly, large, deep-green leaves. Varieties such as 'Golden Queen' (yellow-edged leaves) and 'Silver Queen' (white-edged leaves) make more colourful hedges. 'J.C. van Tol' has almost spineless leaves. Grow well on heavy soils and by the sea. Plant 45cm/18in apart. Trim in late summer.

• **Hornbeam** (*Carpinus betulus*) Deciduous shrub, almost as popular as beech. Large oval leaves, medium green. Like beech, the hornbeam holds on to its dead golden-brown leaves all winter: they are shed as the new leaves unfurl. Quite a fast grower. Grows well on chalky and clay soils; excellent in gardens exposed to cold winds. Plant 45cm/18in apart and trim once a year in late summer.

• **Laurel** (*Prunus laurocerasus*) Evergreen shrub, very large, dark-green glossy leaves. A vigorous grower, soon forming a tall hedge. There is a good variety, 'Rotundifolia', with slightly shorter leaves. Best results in acid soils and sheltered conditions. Plant 60cm/2ft apart and trim any time in summer. Prune with secateurs, as shears or hedge trimmers would cut the large leaves in half and then they go brown at the edges.

• **Privet** (*Ligustrum ovalifolium*) There must be many hundreds of miles of oval-leaved privet grown as hedging, such is its popularity. However, it has serious drawbacks: it needs clipping at least once a month (between mid-spring and late summer) to keep it looking neat, and it is liable to die out suddenly in patches. Privet is a quick grower. Evergreen, or semi-evergreen, oval green leaves. For a bright yellow hedge try growing golden privet ('Aureum'). Both are excellent for exposed gardens and chalky soils, and will tolerate industrial and traffic pollution. Plant 30cm/12in apart.

■ Four formal coniferous hedges

The following conifers, widely used for formal hedging, include one of the fastest-growing hedging plants as well as one of the slowest. All have evergreen foliage.

• **Lawson cypress** (*Chamaecyparis lawsoniana*) Sprays of deep-green foliage, greyish below; variety 'Green Hedger' has rich green foliage. Grows well in exposed windy gardens; recommended for heavy soils. Plant 60cm/2ft apart and trim once a year, in late summer. Quite a fast grower.

• **Leyland cypress** (*Cupressocyparis leylandii*). Extremely fast-growing – under good conditions can put on up to 90cm/3ft of growth in a year. Sprays of deep-green leaves. The variety 'Castlewellan Gold' has yellow foliage, which makes a good bright hedge. Recommended especially for seaside and exposed gardens, and for chalky soils. Plant 60cm/2ft apart and trim in late summer.

• **Western red cedar** (*Thuja plicata* 'Atrovirens'). Bright green shiny foliage carried in flat sprays. Relatively fast grower. Thrives in heavy as well as chalky soils. Plant 60cm/2ft apart and trim in late summer.

• **Yew** (*Taxus baccata*). One of the slowest-growing hedging plants but popular for hundreds of years. Makes a really dense hedge if regularly clipped, and has very deep-green narrow leaves – excellent background to show off colourful plants. Very adaptable, tolerating exposed windy gardens, shade, and heavy and chalky soils. Plant 45cm/18in apart and trim the hedge in late summer.

■ Ten informal flowering and berrying hedges

These shrubs are best grown informally to make the most of their colourful flowers or berries.

• *Berberis darwinii* Evergreen barberry with small holly-like leaves. Whole plant is very prickly. In spring produces masses of deep-yellow flowers, followed by bluish berries. Grows well in chalky soils, a moderately fast grower. Plant 45cm/18in apart and trim back overlong shoots in early summer.

• *Berberis thunbergii* Deciduous, spiny barberry with bright red berries in autumn, when foliage turns to fiery shades. 'Red Chief' and 'Atropurpurea' have reddish-purple foliage, which becomes more colourful in autumn. All are moderately quick growers, ideal for exposed positions, and grow well in chalky or clay soils. Plant 45cm/18in apart and trim back any over-long shoots in early summer.

• *Berberis x stenophylla* Evergreen barberry with deep-green, narrow leaves and very prickly habit. Arching habit of growth. In spring, wreathed with golden-yellow flowers. A moderately fast grower, does well in chalky soils. Plant 45cm/18in apart. Trim back any overlong shoots in early summer.

• **Cotoneaster** (*Cotoneaster* species) Several cotoneasters make good informal hedges: *C. franchetii*, semi-evergreen, heavy crops of orange berries in autumn, plant 45cm/18in apart; *C. lacteus*, evergreen, crops of red berries in autumn, lasting well into winter, plant 45cm/18in apart; *C. simonsii*, semi-evergreen, large red berries in autumn, plant 60cm/2ft apart. All can be grown virtually anywhere: in chalky or clay soils and in coastal gardens. Overlong shoots can be cut back in late summer. All moderately fast growers.

• **Escallonia** (*Escallonia rubra macrantha*) Reasonably fast-growing evergreen shrub. Produces masses of rose-red flowers in summer. Excellent choice for coastal gardens and chalky soils. Plant 60cm/2ft apart and trim back overlong shoots in summer, after flowering is over.

• **Hawthorn** (*Crataegus monogyna*) Described under formal hedges (p14), but also makes a very good informal hedge: will flower and berry freely.

• **Hybrid musk rose** (*Rosa*) Hybrid musks are among the best roses for hedging. Several varieties, including 'Cornelia', 'Felicia' and 'Penelope', with pink, beautifully scented flowers in summer and autumn. Deciduous, fast-growing. Very adaptable, suitable for any fertile well-drained soil, but needs a site in full sun. Plant 45cm/18in apart. Prune back any overlong shoots early in the spring.

• **Ramanas rose** (*Rosa rugosa*) Very spiny, deciduous rose. All varieties recommended for hedging, with pink, red or white single flowers in summer, followed by large orange hips. Fast-growing. Plant 45cm/18in apart. Conditions as for hybrid musk rose. Excellent for coastal gardens.

• **Rhododendron** (*Rhododendron* species) Several species make excellent hedges, including common purple rhododendron, *R. ponticum*: evergreen, with large lanceolate leaves, blooming early summer. Also recommended: the deciduous yellow azalea (*R. luteum*) with scented yellow flowers in late spring and good autumn leaf colour. All rhododendrons need acid or lime-free

soil, and are happy in dappled shade. All are also slow growing. Plant 60cm/2ft apart.

• **Rosemary** (*Rosmarinus officinalis*) Evergreen shrub with
deep-green aromatic foliage and blue flowers in summer. Fast
grower but not good for very exposed or cold gardens. Plant
45cm/18in apart. If necessary prune back overlong shoots in
summer, when flowering is over. 'Miss Jessop's Variety' (or
'Fastigiatus') is recommended too, for its erect habit of growth.

■ **Three informal foliage hedges**

These are grown for their leaves: their flowers are quite
inconspicuous. All have medium-sized leaves.

• **Euonymus** (*Euonymus japonicus*) Evergreen shrub with very
shiny, deep-green oval leaves. Moderately fast grower. Will
thrive in shade, in full sun, in a polluted atmosphere or in
coastal gardens. Also extremely adaptable as regards soils.
Plant 45cm/18in apart. Can also be grown as a formal hedge if
desired; trim in spring or late summer.

• **Field maple** (*Acer campestre*). Deciduous tree. Medium-
green lobed leaves take in attractive yellow tints in autumn
before they fall. Good choice for a natural or country garden.
Moderately fast growing. Plant 45cm/18in apart. Grows particularly well on chalky soils.

• **Griselinia** (*Griselinia littoralis*) Popular hedging plant for seaside gardens: indeed, will only thrive in mild and coastal areas.
Does, however, grow well on chalky soils. Evergreen in these
situations. Large, rounded, leathery, pale-green leaves. Grows
moderately quickly. Plant 60cm/2ft apart. Cut back long or
straggly shoots early summer.

PATHS AND PAVING

**Paved surfaces must be well-drained. When laying
paving materials, begin by excavating 15cm/6in of soil
(which, of course, you can reuse elsewhere). Cover
the area with 10cm/4in of rubble, clinker or small
stones to form a hardcore. Then lay sand or ashes on
top. A camber or gentle tilt will prevent puddles.
Paving around the house should be laid to finish
15cm/6in below the damp-proof course.**

■ **Seven paving materials**

Mixing materials – for example, brick and stone – is effective in moderation. Never use more than two different
kinds, or the effect will be too fussy.

• **Stone flags** Quarried stone is the most expensive choice. If
possible, weather before use. Avoid the cheapest stone substi-
tutes, which are likely to flake within a few years. "Crazy"

paving has irregular gaps in which you can grow creeping plants, such as thyme. This creates an attractive and ornamental path for lightly trodden areas.

• **Concrete slabs** Some have textured finishes, mimicking stone, and some are available in pastel colours. Others are stippled or brushed on one side to create a non-slip finish (ensure this side is uppermost). Some manufacturers issue patterns and laying instructions, and even a package including laying and pointing mortar mixes in dry form: you simply add water. Concrete setts, imitating granite, are also available; being of even depth, they are easier to lay.

• **Brick** Attractively links garden with house if your house has brick walls. Use special paving bricks, which are thinner than wall bricks (and thus easier to lay) and more resistant to frost. A stone edging makes a pleasing contrast. Instead of mortar, you can lay bricks on a sharp sand base with butted joints; only the edging bricks will need to be concreted in.

• **Cobbles** Set in mortar over a hardcore base, using damp (not wet) cobbles to ensure a good bond. Set on their sides, not their ends, for a more comfortable walking surface. Interesting patterns can be made, forming circles within circles, rectangles within rectangles, or a regular, winding flow. But patterns need to be carefully planned out, and cobbles are not quick to lay.

• **Granite setts** Hard cube-shaped stones are expensive but stylish for a regular look. Bed in a dry mix of 5 parts sand to 1 part cement, and allow to set by drawing up moisture from the earth.

• **Concrete** Not to be despised, provided that you give character to the surface by brushing to expose the aggregate before it sets. To strengthen texture further, sprinkle with pebbles. A brick or wood grid will add decorative interest as well as create expansion joints to prevent cracking.

• **Tiles** Historic paving material. Unglazed tiles are preferable: glazed ones become dangerously slippery when wet. Set in mortar laid over hardcore.

■ Seven suggestions for paths

In addition to the paving materials listed above, there are some easier and less expensive alternatives.

• **Gravel** Inexpensive, both to buy and to lay. There are two types. "Binding" gravel has a high proportion of fine materials, which make for a firm surface when compressed. "Clean" gravel – that is, not fixed – promotes security, because you can hear when someone walks over it. With any gravel path, good edgings are necessary – for example, stone, brick or half-buried lengths of timber. Many plants will thrive in gravel.

• **Chamomile** More drought-resistant than grass, and releases a delicious fragrance as you crush it underfoot. Feathery texture attractive. Difficult to weed.

• **Pulverized bark** Rustic feel, good for woodland paths, and increasingly available nowadays.

• **Ashes** Rolled to make a compact path, ashes from a coal fire show off border plants well. Cheap and useful if you have your own source.

• **Old railway sleepers or ties** If available may be laid directly into ground or in bed of gravel. No need for preservative as they are tough and durable.

• **Log rounds or slices** Will have a reasonably long life provided that their surfaces are saw-roughened and they are laid on gravel for good drainage. They should be treated with timber preservative. Excellent when laid randomly in a woodland or wild garden. Can be slippery in wet weather.

• **Stepping stones** Evoke a Japanese mood when laid into a lawn in an irregular line. Set at grass level to allow the mower to pass over. Remember to space them an average step's length apart to make sure that they, and not the lawn, take the wear.

■ Six patterns for brick paths or paving

For complex effects, you can use some bricks with the narrower side exposed, or you can use half-bricks. Bricks are usually designed to have a joint between, but for some patterns you can manage without. The pattern will have a psychological effect, either hurrying you on (as with herringbone, where the continual zig-zag lines follow the path direction) or slowing you down (as with the more static basketweave, suitable for seating areas).

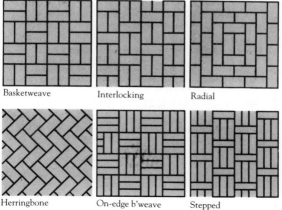

Basketweave   Interlocking   Radial

Herringbone   On-edge b'weave   Stepped

CHANGES OF LEVEL

Changes in level add character to a garden. Where they do not occur naturally you can introduce them, although this can be expensive if soil or other materials have to be either imported or taken away.

■ Three watchpoints when changing level

Be sure that there are adequate access routes for mowers and other equipment between upper and lower levels.

• **Consider drainage** A waterlogged slope may slip, and rainwater may create a bog at the bottom.

• **Avoid steep embankments** These can be difficult to plant, retain and maintain. Even 25° may be too much. A change in level should not obscure the view.

• **Protect trees when earth-moving** Raising or lowering surrounding soil may kill a tree by root suffocation, root exposure or alteration of the water level.

■ Three types of slope

The kind of slope you can create will depend on the size of your garden. .

• **Grass banks** Must be gentle enough for easy mowing. Steep grass slopes can be slippery and cause accidents with mowing equipment. Long grass banks are an alternative to close mowing and look good in a 'wild' garden.

• **Planted slopes** Slopes require hardy plants, tolerant of dry poor conditions, and of sun or shade – depending on aspect. Plant (in prepared pits) more closely than usual to achieve quicker coverage; otherwise, maintenance and weeding will be difficult. Weeds can be suppressed with polythene or a bark mulch until plants have grown enough to provide cover.

• **Terraced slopes** To create a flat area on an existing slope, use the "cut-and-fill" method. First, temporarily remove the topsoil. Then excavate the subsoil and push it further down the embankment to create a level table. Replace the topsoil. This operation is less difficult than cutting into a slope and having to cart away surplus material.

■ Three aspects of step construction

Above all, steps should be safe and permit comfortable ascent or descent. It may be wise to provide a hand rail if the steps are steep or to be used by the infirm.

• **Dimensions** The relationship between risers (vertical faces) and treads (horizontal faces) is critical for the comfort of people walking up or down the steps. Avoid steep risers with shallow treads, or low risers with deep treads. For a given riser

height, work out the tread as follows:
    60cm/2ft – 2 × riser height = tread depth.
Alternatively, for a given tread, use:
    60cm/2ft – tread depth = 2 × riser height.
    In long flights, introduce landings every 10 steps or so.

• **Shadow lines** If possible, allow the tread material to project over the riser by about 2.5cm/1in. The shadow lines caused by such overhangs will define the steps, making them safer.

• **Drainage** The treads must shed rainwater, or ice in winter (and fallen leaves in autumn) will be a hazard.

■ Five materials for steps

Normally, the steps will continue the material of the path which leads to them. However, you may prefer to make the steps stand out with a contrast of colour or texture.

• **Natural stone** Use naturally squarish pieces or incorporate finely dressed treads and risers. Marble is sometimes used but it's very expensive and sometimes not durable in temperate climates. Local stone is generally best.

• **Bricks** As with paving, must be durable, frost-proof and non-slip. It is effective to use a natural stone tread supported by brick risers.

• **Concrete** Blocks finished to look like natural stone are available. If you cast your own concrete *in situ* in a mould, be sure to give a non-slip finish to the tread.

• **Timber** Railway sleepers or ties make excellent steps and are just about the right size if laid on their flat side. Fix with metal or timber stakes to make them stable. You could also use: rough-sawn timber risers with peat, pulverized bark or gravel treads; or logs laid horizontally, fixed with stakes and back-filled with gravel or a lean-mix concrete.

• **Grass** Where the soil is suitable and holds together well, grass gives a lovely soft effect. More suitable for ornament than regular use.

WATER

The sight and sound of water can transform a garden. A lively fountain or stream injects zest and movement, while the still water of a pond evokes calm, tranquillity and relaxation. In small gardens, reflections in water of sky or surrounding plants can increase the sense of space as nothing else can.

■ Five types of garden pond

Avoid siting a pond under a tree: not only will the shade hinder plant growth, but fallen leaves will be harmful to fish and laborious to remove. The best site is a relatively open space sheltered from strong winds. Any pool should be at least 38cm/15in deep, although 45cm/18in is preferable. Create steps or shelves for marginal aquatics where the water is about 23cm/9in deep.

• **Clay** Should be at least 15cm/6in deep and well-puddled (worked with sand to make it impervious to water). Do not allow the clay to dry out before putting water in the pond. Formerly, soot or lime was used beneath the clay to prevent holes being made by worms and other creatures. Today, poly-thene is used instead. The clay must be very plastic and mouldable. Lay with very gently sloping sides. Do not place strong-growing plants (such as willows) too close to the pool edge, or the roots will penetrate the clay and cause leakage.

• **Bentonite** Another natural product. You thoroughly mix this with the prepared inner surface of the proposed pond excava-tion, then rake evenly. On contact with the water, the ben-tonite swells to many times its original size, locking together the soil particles to form an impervious leathery substance. This is inert, so will not harm water life. As with clay, pond sides must be very gentle (not more than 30°) to prevent migration of bentonite particles to bottom. This method is suit-able only with friable or sandy soils with which bentonite will mix; not for use with clay soils. Avoid planting vigorous-rooted plants near edge.

• **Flexible pool liner** Either PVC or butyl. Used mostly for irregular ponds, but will work well with more formal ponds if you provide a supporting framework. A black liner is best, enhancing the mirroring effect of the water surface. Lay liner over a soft base such as raked sand or a manufactured blanket material. A layer of round or smooth gravel, or even earth, on top of the liner will help to prevent puncturing. Don't let the liner show above the water line: tuck beneath surrounding gravel, earth, bricks or paving. Note: polythene is suitable only as a temporary pool liner, as it degrades quickly.

• **Fibreglass** That is, glass-reinforced plastic. Either lay *in situ* within a pre-formed hollow or buy as a ready-made unit and insert in a sand-lined hole. With latter method, excavating right size and shape of hole is more difficult than it sounds. Accurate levelling is essential. Unfortunately, ready-made pools are usually either sky-blue or grey. *In situ* method is a useful option, but calls for a high level of skill.

• **Concrete** Either reinforced blocks or shuttered and poured work. Must be well done, with a dense mass at least 15cm/6in thick, to be impervious. Advisable to finish inside with sand/cement render incorporating waterproofing additive. Harmful chemicals from the concrete may be held in solution for a long time. So treat with a proprietary sealer; or leave for several months, then change water, before putting in plants or fish. Upright sides on formal concrete pools slope very slightly back, so that winter ice will move upwards, not outwards; perfectly straight sides may crack.

■ Four moving water features

I f there is no natural stream, you will need a recirculating pump to create water movement. A submersible pump is usually the best choice. It must be totally covered with water to prevent overheating. Seek expert advice on the best pump size for a particular situation. Employ a qualified electrician to install the system.

• **Fountain** Supplied by pump on floor of pool. Attractive as much for the sound as the sight. Fish will benefit from additional oxygen brought to pond surface by falling water. Place fountain where the jet will catch sunlight and sparkle, and where falling drops will not land on leaves of aquatic plants.

• **Waterfall** Supplied by a length of hose linked to the pump. The pump should be sited as close as possible to the base of the waterfall to increase effectiveness and keep turbulence to a minimum. Looks particularly attractive in a rock garden. Steps 15–30cm/6–12in in height are adequate for good visual impact. Pre-formed fibreglass cascades are available, but they tend to look unnatural.

• **Millstone feature** Water is pumped through the central hold of the millstone so that it spills out all around the circumference. May be either a real millstone or textured fibreglass, available in various sizes as part of a complete millstone kit. A reservoir below the stone houses the pump. An attractive water feature for a small garden, with no danger to young children.

• **Bubble fountain** Another safe feature for a garden used by children. Simply an arrangement of boulders and pebbles laid over a flexible liner with a reservoir beneath from which water is pumped – either through a simple water jet or via a special fountainhead unit. The pebbles lie on supporting metal mesh to keep them above the reservoir.

PATIOS

These are principally places to sit, relax – and perhaps entertain. The planting is often dominated by container plants and climbers, the latter trained on trelliswork to form an attractive floral screen, perhaps against a wall of the house.

■ Four considerations when planning a patio

A bove all, the sitting area should be flat, making walking comfortable and ensuring that tables and chairs will not rock around. There should be space enough to accommodate garden furniture (perhaps a table and seating for four), with plenty left over for people to move around.

• **Aspect** In temperate climates the sitting area will often be positioned to form a suntrap; in hot climates a shady retreat. Where a house faces north (south in southern hemisphere), a patio close by is likely to be in shade; consider siting the patio away from the house in a sunny spot, reserving a small shady area for really hot weather.

• **Drainage** A fall of about 2.5cm/1in in 3.6m/12ft, away from the house, is enough to shed surface water. A patio should finish 15cm/6in below any adjacent damp-proof course. Consider using smooth round gravel for a self-draining patio.

• **Transition areas** It is a good idea to introduce some "foundation" planting between the patio and house wall; without it, the visual effect can sometimes be too severe. Use hanging baskets, window boxes or floor-standing container plants to create a planted "garden" area.

• **Furniture** Chairs and tables are available in a range of materials, including aluminium alloy, cast iron, reconstituted stone, wood or plastic. Robust timber seats can remain outdoors all year round if coated in timber preservative every 2–3 years. Other furniture may have to be brought inside – check that it dismantles or folds away easily, unless you are unusually well-off for storage space.

■ Eight types of containers

Pots and containers come in a vast range of materials and styles. The shape of any planter (but especially the rigid forms) should allow for frozen soil or compost to expand upwards, thus avoiding damage. Pots should be at least 20cm/8in in diameter or the soil will dry out too quickly in bright sunshine or may freeze solid in winter. Put heavy containers in position before you fill them. Place a pot on a stand of bricks if there is a risk of drainage holes becoming blocked. Put in a layer of crocks or coarse gravel at the bottom of the container, then fill with compost.

• **Clay-terracotta pots** Arguably the best material for containers. Controls soil temperatures and water retention most evenly. Choose a suitable type of pot: not all pots are frost-resistant. White or green deposits can be removed with a scrubbing brush and water. Urn-shaped and amphora-shaped pots have a classical feel.

• **Timber planters** The life of timber containers should be extended by lining with polythene, bitumen paint or zinc. Good drainage is essential. Oak barrels sawn in half are frequently sold: check that the hoops are securely attached and the wooden section held firm.

• **Plastic pots** Very lightweight but can discolour and become brittle with time, unless treated during manufacture to resist degradation by sunlight. Ideal, filled with a peat-based compost, for roof gardens, where weight is crucial.

• **Stone troughs and urns** Can look superb in the right setting. Very heavy, so position with care. Antique urns (highly priced) are sold by certain specialists. Even reproduction versions made of reconstituted stone are expensive.

• **Concrete troughs** Heavy, but can be attractive. Reinforced concrete planters can break down in severe weather if their reinforcing bars begin to rust. Some concrete containers are supplied with removable liners, useful for changing bedding schemes with minimum effort.

• **Window boxes** Wooden or plastic. Proprietary plastic types may not have enough draining holes, so drill more if necessary. Choose subdued colours. Boxes should be at least 15cm/6in wide and 20cm/8in deep and should be fitted with 2 or more feet to hold them 2.5–6cm/1–2in above the windowsill so that excess water drains off.

• **Hanging baskets** Good for brightening up walls and entrances. They tend to dry out more quickly than pots, tubs and boxes, so water twice a day in warm weather. Some plastic baskets have a built-in drip tray. For open-mesh baskets the traditional lining material is sphagnum moss.

• **Improvised containers** Old chimney pots are especially attractive. You could also use an old sink or even a cast-iron fireplace. Wooden wheelbarrows also offer possibilities.

TOOLS AND TECHNIQUES

TOOLS

It is better to buy just a few tools of good quality than a vast selection of cheap implements that will be uncomfortable to use, short-lived and of little practical value. Although a good spade or fork is not cheap, with care (cleaned and hung up after use) it will probably have as long a life as its owner.

■ **Six basic tools**

These are the essential tools, used during soil cultivation, sowing and planting.

• **Fork** For digging heavy soils, breaking down rough-dug soil and for light surface cultivation. The head of a full-size four-tine fork measures 30.5 x 19cm/12 x 7½in; that of a small border fork measures 23 x 14cm/9 x 5½in.

• **Hoe** For surface cultivation, particularly to eradicate weeds between rows of plants. There are two basic types: the Dutch Hoe, which cuts horizontally through the soil; and the Draw Hoe, which is used with a chopping action (particularly recommended for stony or heavy soils, and also for making seed drills). Both have 1.5m/5ft handles.

• **Rake** Most useful is the 30cm/12in wide steel rake with teeth 5cm/2in apart and a 1.5m/5ft long handle. Used for levelling soil and for creating a fine tilth for seed sowing.

• **Spade** For digging and for planting (eg trees and shrubs). The standard spade blade measures 29 x 19cm/11½ x 7½in; that of the lady's spade 25 x 16.5cm/10 x 6½in; and that of the border spade 23 x 14cm/9 x 5½in. Heavy digging is easiest with middle size. Shaft should have a gentle crank (or curve) above blade to allow maximum leverage.

• **Trowel** The short-handled hand trowel is invaluable for planting small plants and bulbs. Handle is 10–15cm/4–6in long. Longer handles are sometimes available.

• **Wheelbarrow** In larger gardens and on the vegetable plot a wheelbarrow can save a lot of time and energy. When choosing a model, make sure that the bulk of the load is placed over the wheel. A ball-wheeled barrow is easier to push over soft ground, and is less likely to damage the ground. A two-wheeled barrow is easier to load and push than one with a single wheel. Stout planks are useful for wheeling up steps.

■ Seven tools for the keen gardener

The following tools are not essential for successful gardening, but they do help you to do a really good job. Garden items such as lines, dibbers and measuring rods can easily be made at home.

• **Cultivator** This has a curved fork-like head on a 1.2m/4ft shaft and is used to cultivate and aerate the soil to a depth of several inches between rows of vegetables. An ideal tool for hard or stony soils.

• **Dibber** Used for making planting holes quickly, particularly for vegetables such as cabbages and leeks. It looks like the top 30cm/12in of a spade handle and has a pointed tip. (Indeed, you could make your own from an old spade handle.)

• **Hand fork** 3- or 4-pronged hand forks are useful for transplanting seedlings, for working among tightly packed plants and for intricate planting and weeding.

• **Line** A stout nylon or hemp garden line is useful to the vegetable gardener when planting/sowing in straight rows. Best if the twine is wound on a special steel reel. Lines wound around stout stakes are easy to make at home.

• **Measuring rod** Invaluable on the vegetable plot for measuring the distance between plants when planting out or thinning (and for any other plant spacing). Made from a piece of straight 2.5cm/1in square timber, marked off every 10 and 5cm, plus 1cm graduations in the first 30cm (or every 12, 6 and 3in, plus 1in gradations in the first foot).

• **Onion hoe** Small short-handled version of the draw hoe, ideal for thinning out seedlings, and cultivating and weeding between closely spaced rows and plants.

• **Sprayer** A garden pressure sprayer is used for applying pesticides and weedkillers. (A jet of pure water will dislodge aphids.) Be sure to observe the rules of safety. Various capacities are available. Should have an adjustable nozzle. A small hand sprayer is more convenient in the greenhouse.

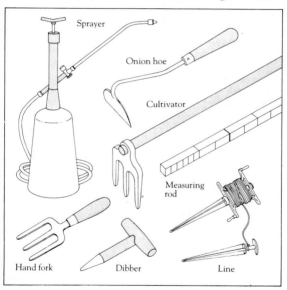

Sprayer

Onion hoe

Cultivator

Measuring rod

Hand fork   Dibber   Line

■ Eight useful cutting tools

Here is a selection of garden tools used for pruning, cutting hedges and grass, plant propagation and other tasks of this nature.

• **Knife** A straight-bladed horticultural knife is useful for cutting string and for taking cuttings. Don't choose one with a stainless-steel blade, as this quickly becomes blunt.

• **Long-arm pruner** Has a very long shaft (at least 2.4m/8ft) with a cutting blade at the top, operated by a lever at the bottom. Invaluable for high branches.

• **Pruners** (or loppers) These have two long handles and are essential for "heavy" pruning – that is, stems of 1.25–2.5cm/ ½–1in in diameter.

• **Pruning saw** Used on large branches where loppers or secateurs are inadequate. Usually has a narrow curved blade.

• **Scythe** Tool with a curved blade and a long shaft with two handles. The blade may be long (for cutting grass) or short (for brambles and so on).

• **Secateurs** Used for all general pruning, provided that stems are not too thick. Those with a scissor action are recommended. There are lightweight, medium and heavy-duty models.

• **Sickle** For cutting long grass, cutting down weeds, and similar tasks. Resembles a short-handled scythe.

• **Shears** For hedge trimming, cutting long grass around trees, and lightly trimming over plants to remove dead flower heads (such as heather and lavender). Make sure they are comfortable to hold.

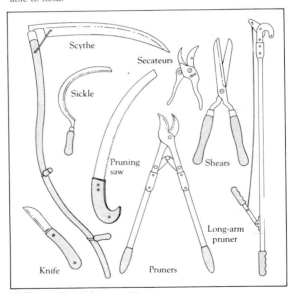

■ Eleven lawn care tools

There are numerous tools which are designed for use on lawns.

• **Aerator** The hollow-tine fork removes plugs of soil to aerate the lawn; ideal for heavy soils.

• **Besom** A broom made of birch twigs. Ideal for sweeping up leaves and working top-dressings into the lawn. Hold a besom almost level with the ground and make broad sweeps with it.

• **Dribble bar** A bar-shaped sprinkler attached to the spout of a watering can to apply weedkillers and other solutions evenly.

• **Edging shears** Shears with long handles for cutting along the edges of a lawn.

• **Fertilizer distributor** A wheeled hand-propelled implement with a hopper, used for spreading fertilizers evenly. Many are quite inexpensive.

• **Half-moon iron** Has a semi-circular blade on a long handle. Used for cutting turf prior to lifting, and also for re-cutting ragged and damaged lawn edges.

• **Lute** Can be made at home by fixing a pair of long handles to a 1.5–1.8m/5–6ft long plank of wood (on edge), to form a giant "rake". Used to work in top-dressings.

• **Roller** A plastic roller filled with water is adequate for lawns.

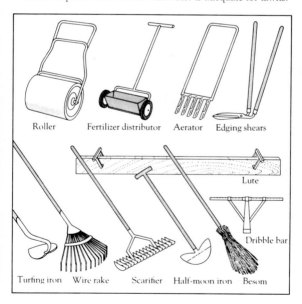

Roller   Fertilizer distributor   Aerator   Edging shears

Lute

Dribble bar

Turfing iron   Wire rake   Scarifier   Half-moon iron   Besom

• **Scarifier** Resembles a rake but has half-moon disks instead of tines. Used to remove moss, rake in fertilizer and aerate the soil. An alternative is the wire lawn rake.

• **Turfing iron** Rather like a spade but has a heart-shaped blade on a curved neck. Used for lifting turf.

• **Wire lawn rake (or spring-tine rake)** Fan-shaped with long springy teeth of heavy-gauge wire. Used for general lawn raking and for light scarifying.

■ Four power tools

These may be useful for owners of large gardens, to cut down on time and effort.

• **Chain saw** Good for heavy pruning and tree felling. Electrically powered chain saws are much lighter than their petrol-driven counterparts and are thus easier and safer to use.

• **Hedge trimmer** Makes light work of long tall hedges. There are electric and petrol-driven models, the latter for really heavy work. The 45cm–60cm/18–24in blade may be single- or double-sided: the latter is preferable.

• **Rotary cultivator** Turns the soil over by steel blades rotating on a central spindle. There are both large and small models, all self-propelled. The larger machines generally cultivate to great depths. Useful for large neglected areas.

• **Trimmer** Powered trimmers are in vogue. A rapidly rotating nylon cord, or various types of blades, cut long grass, weeds or brambles. Lightweight electric trimmers are suitable for grass, while petrol-driven models are best for tougher work.

■ Five watering aids

Most of these aids enable the garden to be watered while you get on with something else – or simply relax!

• **Hose pipe** Most useful if fitted with a sprinkler, drip irrigation or perforated hose (see below). Buy a strong hose pipe which will not kink when bent. A hose storage reel will keep the hose pipe neat and tidy when it is not in use.

• **Drip irrigation** Lengths of pipe fitted with short drip nozzles, or with longer "spaghetti"tubes, which can be directed to individual plants in the garden or greenhouse. A lot of plants can thus be watered simultaneously, at the turn of a tap.

• **Perforated hose** A lay-flat perforated hose distributes a fine spray of water among plants.

• **Sprinkler** There are two main types, both of which are attached to a hose pipe: the rotating type, and the oscillating type which moves backwards and forwards, producing a square or rectangular spray pattern. Sprinklers are especially useful for watering lawns.

• **Watering can** A 9-litre/2-gallon watering can will be found most useful for general garden needs. Use this for container plants and for watering in newly planted subjects. Spray heads of "roses" are supplied with most cans.

■ Five types of mower

The large range of lawn mowers available falls into two basic categories: cylinder and rotary.

• **Cylinder mower, manual** Blades are attached to a cylinder which revolves horizontally against a fixed blade. Cylinder mowers provide a fine, even cut on good turf but are no use on rough ground. There are side-wheel models and rear-roller models: the latter give a striped effect. A mower with a 5- or 6-bladed cylinder is suitable only for coarse lawns; more blades are needed for fine lawns. Various cutting widths are available. Most cylinder mowers have a grassbox to collect the clippings: you should use this.

• **Cylinder mower, powered** Petrol engine, battery or mains electricity. Again, not suitable for rough ground. Some power mowers are self-propelled, others have to be pushed as only the cylinder is powered. The former are recommended for large lawns. Where an exceptionally fine cut is required a mower with a 10- or 12-bladed cylinder is recommended.

• **Rotary mower, self-propelled** For cutting rough grass, including banks, this is the best choice. Blades rotating at high speed slash the grass, rather like a scythe. Some models are equipped with grassboxes or bags, others are not. Self-propelled rotaries have either wheels or rollers. Petrol or electric, the latter for small grass areas. Rotaries are not intended for use on fine lawns. Some models are supplied with a grassbox, which you should make a habit of using.

• **Rotary mower, hand-propelled** Only the blades are powered, so you have to push the machine. Recommended only for small areas of grass.

• **Hover mower** Works on the rotary principle (see above) but instead of being supported on wheels it hovers on a cushion of air. Electric or petrol-driven. Very easy to use. Recommended for utility lawns. Some hovers come with a grassbox.

■ Three hints on buying tools

Buying tools is like buying anything else: you only get what you pay for. Don't be tempted by false economy.

• **Quality of steel** With cutting tools, such as knives, secateurs or saws, you should shop at the top end of the market. On cheap cutting tools the steel will be soft and of poor quality, so that cutting edges will soon become blunt, and quickly worn away by sharpening. Likewise, spades and forks of good-quality forged steel will last a lifetime.

• **Stainless steel** Spades, forks, rakes, hoes, hand forks, trowels and other tools of this type are available in stainless steel versions. These are far more expensive than tools in forged steel but they are long-lasting, penetrate the soil more easily and soil is less likely to stick to them. Do not choose stainless steel knife blades, however; they quickly become blunt and are difficult to sharpen.

• **Shafts and handles** Shafts are made from several different materials. Wood is traditional and long-lasting: make sure that the wood is close grained and that the grain runs down the length of the shaft. Shafts made from polypropylene are light-weight yet strong. Lighter tools such as hoes and rakes are often equipped with aluminium, alloy sheets coated with plastic. Spades and forks are fitted with handles in three shapes: T, D and YD. If possible try all three before choosing.

■ Six aspects of tool care

Thoroughly clean gardening tools and machines after use so that they remain in good working order. Dirty tools can mean harder work.

• **Hand tools** After use, brush or scrape hand tools free of soil, then (unless they are of stainless steel) rub over blades with an oily rag to prevent rust formation.

• **Mowers** After use, clear away grass cuttings. Clean with a stiff hand brush and remove any long stems from around cylinder or rotor spindle. Undersides of rotary mowers may become rusty if left dirty. Wash clean, rub down any rust with emery paper and rub metal surfaces with an oily rag. Regular lubrication is important – follow maintenance instructions in the handbook.

• **Power tools** Cultivators should be oiled and greased after use. Carry out regular maintenance as described in handbook. Keep rotor blades clean and lightly oiled. Give similar treatment to hedge trimmers, chain saws and powered trimmers.

• **Servicing** Follow manufacturer's instructions regarding the servicing of lawn mowers, cultivators and other machines and powered equipment. Correct sharpening and adjustment once a year will help to ensure many years of life. During the winter inspect machines for rust on painted surfaces. If rust is present, rub down painted areas thoroughly with emery paper, prime any bare metal, then apply a paint recommended for metal surfaces.

• **Sharpening** Few gardeners think of sharpening a hoe or spade but both tools will cut better if their edges are kept keen. Use a file to hone up leading edge of blade. Knives and secateurs should always have a really keen edge: use an oilstone for best results. Only sharpen the factory-sharpened edge. (The job can be done professionally if you prefer.)

• **Storage** Store all tools and machines in a dry shed or garage. Provide a rack or a series of hooks for tools to keep them tidy.

Keep metal parts of all tools in store lightly coated with oil or grease. Before storing a petrol-driven machine, empty the tank.

SOIL CULTIVATION AND CARE

Inadequate soil preparation before planting or sowing is a major cause of horticultural disappointment. Digging and the application of fertilizers and bulky organic materials are usually necessary to ensure that the soil is suited to the plants or crops that you want to grow. Drainage may also be required.

■ Four fertilizers that supply all the major foods.

There are certain fertilizers that supply all three of the principal foods required by plants: nitrogen for leaf and stem growth; phosphorus for good root growth; potassium (potash), which helps to form and ripen flowers, fruits and seeds.

• **Blood, fish and bone** Slowly releases nitrogen, phosphorus and potash; use before sowing or planting, or around established plants.

• **Fishmeal** Dig in before planting or sowing in spring.

• **Compound fertilizer** Popular general fertilizer, suitable for use as a complete plant food. NPK (Nitrogen/Phosphorus/Potassium) ratio is quoted on each manufacturer's product.

• **Seaweed meal** Dried seaweed. Contains large amounts of potash and nitrogen, and some phosphorus. Fork into soil around plants during spring and summer.

■ Twelve fertilizers that supply specific food

In addition to nitrogen, phosphorus and potash, there are several other foods that plants need in smaller amounts, such as magnesium and iron.

• **Basic slag** Slowly provides phosphorus to the soil. Can be applied in autumn or winter before digging. Improves texture and drainage of heavy soils.

• **Bonemeal** Popular for adding to soil before planting, especially trees and shrubs. By no means essential. Supplies phosphorus and a small amount of nitrogen.

• **Dried blood** Rich in nitrogen and quick-acting. Apply around plants in spring and summer.

• **Hoof and horn meal** Supplies nitrogen over a long period. Use as bonemeal.

• **Lime** Supplies calcium and increases the pH of soils. You often need to apply this to acid soils, especially on the vegetable plot, to bring the pH up to a suitable level: around 6.5 – 7.0. Ascertain pH with a simple soil-testing kit. Apply lime (eg in the form of hydrated lime or ground limestone) in autumn or winter after digging.

• **Magnesium sulphate** Best-known as Epsom salts. Corrects magnesium deficiency in plants (yellowing leaves). Dilute in water (65g per litre/½oz per gallon). Apply in spring or summer by watering soil or spraying foliage.

• **Nitrate of soda** Supplies nitrogen; very quick-acting. Use as growth booster in spring/summer around established plants, applying as topdressing.

• **Nitro-chalk** Supplies nitrogen and calcium. Useful on acid soils. Apply in spring/summer before sowing or planting, or as topdressing around established plants.

• **Sequestered iron** Supplies iron. Water in around plants in spring or summer. Valuable in lime or chalk soils.

• **Sulphate of ammonia** Supplies nitrogen – quick-acting. Use before sowing or planting, or as topdressing in spring or summer to encourage leafy growth.

• **Sulphate of potash** Quickly supplies potash. Encourages flowering and fruiting. Use as sulphate of ammonia.

• **Superphosphate of lime** Supplies phosphorus. Use as sulphate of ammonia.

■ Twelve bulky organic materials

Although most of these supply some plant foods, their main role is to improve soils – to make them more moisture-retentive (especially light sandy types) and to help improve drainage (especially heavy clay soils). Add to the trenches during digging.

• **Bark** Pulverized bark is available with or without added fertilizers. It lasts a long time in the soil. Good as a surface mulch. Apply 2–4kg per sq metre/5–10lb per sq yard. Give a dusting of sulphate of ammonia at the same time to replace that used by bacteria in breaking down the bark.

• **Farmyard manure** Contains foods in varying amounts. One of the best soil improvers. Use it well-rotted. Apply 6kg per sq metre/15lb per sq yard.

• **Garden compost** Valuable alternative to farmyard manure, good soil conditioner and quite high in plant foods; apply 4 kg per sq metre/10lb per sq yard. See pp37–8.

• **Green manure** Method of improving soil by sowing certain crops (such as rape) and then digging them into the ground. Suitable for vegetable plot.

• **Hop manure** Spent hops (see below) plus fertilizers. Use sparingly – 0.4kg per sq metre/1lb per sq yard.

• **Leafmould** Leaves of deciduous trees, collected in autumn and stacked (in an open position), can be returned to the soil in one or two year's time, after they have broken down to a crumbly dark brown mould. Apply at a rate of 2kg per sq metre/5lb per sq yard.

• **Mushroom compost** Spent composts sold off by mushroom growers. Contain varying amounts of food, plus chalk (don't use if you intend to grow rhododendrons and other lime-haters). Apply 2–4kg per sq metre/5–10lb per sq yard.

• **Peat** Popular soil improver, but supplying little or no plant foods. Apply 4kg per sq metre/10lb per sq yard. It must be moist. One consideration of the fact that peat is a non-renewable resource should govern the use of peat in the garden. There are acceptable alternatives now available from renewable sources, such as coco fibre.

• **Poultry manures** Use well-rotted. High in foods. Apply 4–6kg per sq metre/10–15lb per sq yard.

• **Seaweed** Often available in coastal areas. Use fresh or composted. High in plant foods. Apply about 4kg per sq metre/10lb per sq yard.

• **Sewage sludge (dried)** Availability limited. Not particularly high in organic matter but contains good supply of nitrogen and some phosphates. Apply 0.6–1kg per sq metre/1½–2½lb per sq yard.

• **Spent hops** By-product of the brewing industry. Contains few foods but good soil conditioner. Apply 4kg per sq metre/10lb per sq yard.

■ Five ways to cultivate the soil

Digging is usually necessary to incorporate bulky organic materials, relieve compaction, improve drainage, improve soil texture and control growth of weeds.

• **Single digging** Type of digging in which the soil is cultivated to the depth of the spade blade. The most widely practised form of digging, adequate for most ordinary soils of reasonable

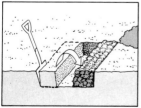 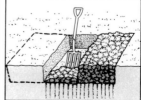

depth which do not overlay an intractable subsoil. First, take out a trench one blade deep, then fill this in using adjacent soil, turning each spadeful upsidedown as you do. As you move in this way across the areas of ground, the trench moves with you. Soil from the first trench is used to fill the final one at the other end of the plot.

• **Double digging** Digging soil to two depths of the spade. Especially useful on land which has not been cultivated before or where a hard subsoil layer is impeding drainage and the penetration of plant roots.

• **Forking** On very heavy or very stony ground, which is difficult to penetrate with a spade. You may use a fork instead. Also may be better for breaking up soil in the bottom of trenches during double digging. And you can use a fork to good effect as a cultivating tool between established plants, and to break down rough-dug ground in spring.

• **Raking** To level a piece of ground for seed sowing or planting. Creates a fine tilth for sowing into. Don't create a tilth as fine as dust, though, or the soil surface will pan in the first shower of rain.

• **Rotation** Growing vegetables on a different section of the plot each year, in a three-year cycle, to prevent build-up of pests and diseases. Divide the plot into three sections: one for legumes (peas, beans and suchlike) and salads, one for root crops (carrots, etc) and one for brassicas (cabbages, etc). The section which has brassicas one year will grow root crops in the 2nd, followed by legumes in the 3rd. In the 4th year it will be used to grow brassicas again.

■ Three ways to drain wet soil

If cultivation such as double-digging does not improve soil drainage – that is, if the soil still lies waterlogged over the winter – then you will need to install a drainage system. Each of the systems described below should be connected to a soakaway at the lowest point of the garden: dig a hole at least 1.8m/6ft in diameter and depth, line it with uncemented concrete blocks, fill with rubble and top with turf. Excess water collects here and then drains to lower levels.

• **Ditches** The cheapest method: dig ditches to carry excess water from the cultivated soil to soakaway. They should be 0.9–1.2m/3–4ft deep with the sides sloping outwards at a 20–30° angle.

• **Land drains** Land or tile drains are short sections of earthenware or longer sections of plastic pipe laid end to end, usually in a herringbone system of sloping filled trenches. The system leads to a soakaway. Installing land drains is a major investment, but well worthwhile in large, badly drained areas.

• **Rubble drains** On small sites where ditches and tile drains would be impractical, use rubble drains – trenches filled with rubble capped with a layer of gravel. Replace topsoil.

■ Three ways to improve difficult soils

These are soils which may dry out excessively in summer, or soils which lie wet in winter and are difficult to work in spring. Often, the same soil displays both characteristics.

• **Clay soil** A heavy, often wet and cold sticky soil. Add plenty of grit or coarse horticultural sand to the trenches during digging and mix these materials in the topsoil. Apply lime in autumn after digging unless the soil pH is above 7.0, in which case apply horticultural gypsum. Both these take the stickiness out of clay soils, making them easier to work in spring. Bulky organic matter adds humus, so incorporate plenty during digging to give you a more crumbly texture.

• **Sandy soil** Extremely light and free draining; can become excessively dry in summer. Poor in plant foods. During digging add plenty of bulky organic matter, which helps to conserve soil moisture. Mulch plants with organic matter. Always apply fertilizers before sowing or planting, and as topdressing in spring/summer. Dense planting will stop soil erosion in exposed windy gardens. Lime will be needed if the soil is very acid (not for lime-hating plants, of course), especially on the vegetable plot.

• **Chalky soils** Topsoil is often very shallow; poor in plant food. Can dry out excessively in summer. Use plenty of bulky organic matter when digging, especially acid types such as peat. Organic matter is inclined to disappear quickly, so needs to be used regularly, in large quantities. Mulch with it, too. Always apply fertilizers, as for sandy soils.

■ Four steps in making and using good garden compost

Garden compost is the next best thing to farmyard manure. There are many materials that can be composted – that is, formed into a heap and rotted down.

• **Setting up the bins** To retain the heap of compost material construct a wire-netting enclosure 1.2m/4ft high, 1.2m/4ft wide and any length you wish. Alternatively, use a proprietary compost bin. It's best to have two compost heaps: one for immediate use, the other in the process of rotting.

• **Choosing the compostable materials** Mix the various materials together before adding them to the heap. You can use annual weeds, lawn mowings, potato peelings, animal manure, torn-up newspaper, soft hedge clippings, vegetable leaves and stems, tree and shrub leaves, and many other kinds of soft material – but not hard woody stuff such as fruit-tree prunings. In a separate wire bin you can also rot down deciduous leaves on their own to make soil-enriching leafmould.

• **Constructing the heap** Place a 15–23cm/6–9in layer of slightly moist compost material in the bin. Lightly firm it down. Scatter sulphate of ammonia over this layer at the rate of 12g per sq metre/½oz to the sq yard, then add another layer of compost material. Continue in this fashion until the bin is full. Keep a cover over the top of the heap at all times. You can alternate the layer of sulphate of ammonia with one of lime to counteract acidity. Alternatively, you can use a proprietary compost activator between each layer.

• **Using the compost** Decomposition is more rapid in spring and summer than in autumn and winter. A good heap should be ready to use within 6 months of being completed. The compost should be brown and crumbly. Allow a year or even 2 years for leafmould. Dig in compost at 4kg per sq metre/10lb per sq yard.

■ Seven ways to suppress weeds

Weeds must be kept under control for they compete with cultivated plants for food, moisture, air and light. A dense weed cover between plants can seriously retard growth.

• **Hand weeding** Small areas, rock gardens and the like can be weeded by hand. Use a hand fork to lightly loosen the soil, then pull out the weeds including roots. With perennial weeds, such as dandelions, you will have to dig deeper, as their roots are long. Weeds come out more easily after rain.

• **Hoeing and cultivating** In the vegetable and flower garden you can kill seedling weeds by hoeing regularly, using a Dutch or draw hoe. Choose a warm, dry day, when the soil surface is dry. A cultivator hoe drawn through the soil regularly will serve the same purpose (as well as prevent surface panning).

• **Spot weeding** Treatment of individual perennial weeds (such as dandelions, docks or bindweed) with a weedkiller in aerosol or stick form. Only feasible where few weeds are present. Useful for flower borders and lawns. Mostly the weedkiller glyphosate is used. For lawns use a selective weedkiller.

• **Weedkillers** You can kill most weeds with just a few of the many different chemical weedkillers available in garden centres. Paraquat is useful for killing annual weeds on bare ground, or between shrubs, fruits and so on if used carefully; do not allow it to come in contact with foliage of cultivated plants. The same warning applies to glyphosate, which controls a wide range of perennial weeds. Certain weedkillers can be applied to completely weed-free soil between cultivated plants to prevent germination of weed seeds for many weeks (dichlobenil granules) or many months (simazine). The soil must not be disturbed after application. With all weedkillers, carefully follow manufacturers' instructions or you could damage or kill valued plants.

• **Organic mulches** Bulky organic materials, such as well-rotted farmyard manure, garden compost, leafmould, spent hops, pulverized bark and mushroom compost, can be used to cover the soil around permanent plants. This technique, known as mulching, suppresses annual weeds and helps to conserve soil moisture in dry weather. Apply a mulch in spring to completely weed-free, moist soil, about 6–8cm/2–3in deep. Top up as necessary in spring.

• **Polythene mulching** Sheets of black mulching polythene laid over the soil, with edges buried in the soil, will suppress annual weeds. A technique for the vegetable or fruit garden. Lay sheets between rows; or lay a large sheet first and plant vegetables (such as brassicas, strawberries and lettuces) through holes made at regular intervals.

• **Mineral mulches** In certain ornamental areas, such as the rock garden or beds of permanent plants around a patio, you can permanently cover the soil surface with a decorative layer of pea shingle, about 1.25–2.5cm/½–1in deep. Suppresses annual weeds and helps conserve soil moisture in dry weather.

PROPAGATION

Raising your own plants is much cheaper than buying from a nursery or garden centre. Although a greenhouse is helpful if you want to raise tender plants, a cold frame also has plenty of possibilities for propagating plants.

■ Six propagating aids

Apart from a greenhouse and cold frame, there are various other tools and materials which you will find useful for the successful propagation of plants.

• **Cutting compost** Used for rooting cuttings. Made at home by mixing equal parts by bulk of moist sphagnum moss peat and coarse horticultural sand. Alternatively use equal parts peat or coco fibre and perlite.

• **Seed compost** The best compost for sowing seeds – provided that it is fresh. Buy as you need it from a garden centre. You can use either traditional loam-based seed compost (such as John Innes) or a soilless (all-peat) type.

• **Hormone rooting powder** You dip bases of cuttings in this before inserting them in the compost. Speeds rooting, results in a strong root system, and encourages "difficult" subjects to produce roots – such as camellias and rhododendrons.

• **Peat pellets** Bought as dry compressed disks. When soaked in water they swell up to produce 4 x 4cm/1⅝ x 1⅝in cylinders which you can use for sowing single, large seeds (such as sweet peas) or for rooting cuttings. The seed (or cutting) is sown in the central hole and covered with seed compost. The pellets are potted or planted with the young plant so its roots are not disturbed.

• **Propagator** An electrically heated propagating case is extremely useful for germinating seeds and for rooting cuttings. Types vary from very small windowsill propagators which cost only a few pence per week to run, to large sophisticated greenhouse kinds which hold a number of seed trays. All are heated by warming cables sealed in the base; these provide a temperature of around 18–21°C/65–70°F, necessary for most seeds and cuttings.

• **Seed trays** For sowing larger quantities of seeds and for rooting sizeable batches of cuttings. Standard-size plastic seed trays measure 38 x 23cm/15 x 9in and depths range from 2.5cm/1in to 8cm/3in. Fill with seed or cutting compost and use the shallowest trays for seed sowing, the deepest for pricking out seedlings and rooting cuttings.

■ Two ways to raise plants from seeds outdoors

Hardy annuals, hardy perennials and most vegetables can be sown directly out of doors.

• **Broadcast sowing** A method not often used except for grass seed, and perhaps for large patches of vegetables such as carrots and radishes. All you do is scatter the seeds evenly over a finely prepared seed bed, then lightly rake them into the soil surface. Finally, you lightly firm down the soil by tapping all over with the back of a rake.

• **Sowing in drills** Normal method of sowing, whether vegetable seeds or bold groups of hardy annuals. A drill is simply a straight shallow furrow, which you can make by drawing a pointed stick, or the corner of a draw hoe, through the soil, using a garden line as a guide, as illustrated in the first diagram

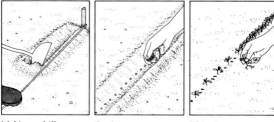

Making a drill   Sowing   Thinning

below. Depth is important and varies according to size of seeds. For average-size seeds such as carrots and lettuce make drills about 1.25cm/½in deep. Next, take a "pinch" of seeds between finger and thumb and trickle evenly and thickly along the drill, making sure none are touching. Then carefully rake soil over them and firm lightly with back of rake.

■ Two tasks to perform after sowing

eep an eye on the growing seedlings. If they are allowed to grow too close together they may become weak and spindly, so that proper growth is hindered.

• **Transplanting seedlings** Seedlings of some plants need transplanting, either to their final sites or to nursery beds for growing on. Examples are members of the cabbage family and spring bedding plants such as wallflowers. When seedlings are about 8cm/3in high carefully lift them with a hand fork and replant in holes made with a hand trowel or dibber. Firm them in well with a heel or hands and water them in.

• **Thinning seedlings** Seedlings of some plants must not be transplanted, but to give them room to grow they may need thinning out. Examples are hardy annuals, carrots, radishes, beetroots and parsnips. Carry out thinning as soon as seedlings are large enough to handle easily. You can chop out surplus seedlings with a draw hoe. Alternatively, carefully pull them out, making sure you firm soil around remaining ones with your fingers. It's a good idea to water the remaining seedlings with a watering can with a rose fitment or sprinkler to settle the soil around them.

■ Five steps in raising plants from seeds indoors

he following method is suitable for either a greenhouse or a windowsill. Although the instructions below apply specifically to sowing in seed trays, the method is basically the same when you use pots – except that you will need a round wooden presser.

• **Preparing the compost** Fill the tray to overflowing with seed compost and scrape off surplus until compost is level with top. Firm all over with fingers, then press firmly with a wooden presser of a size to fit the tray. This should give you a smooth level surface.

• **Sowing the seeds** In the palm of one hand hold enough seeds for the tray. Raise this hand 10–15cm/4–6in above the tray and move it to and fro across the compost surface, at the same time gently tapping it with your other hand to slowly release the seeds so that they scatter evenly. (Some people sow directly from the packet, but this gives less control.) Sow half the quantity of seeds in one direction and the other half at right angles. To ensure even sowing of very fine dust-like seeds (such as lobelia and begonia) mix with a quantity of very fine dry silver sand; this makes handling easier.

• **Covering the seeds** Do this by sifting an even layer of compost over them, using a fine or medium sieve. This layer of compost should be equal to twice diameter of seeds. Fine dust-like seeds must not be covered.

Preparing the compost

Sowing the seeds

Covering the seeds

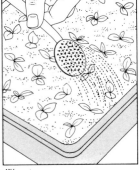
Watering

• **Watering and storage** Stand trays in water after sowing and leave until surface of compost becomes moist. (Or water compost surface with a watering can fitted with a fine rose.) Then place in warmth – for example, in a propagator.

• **Pricking out** Transplanting seedlings to other trays or pots to give them room to grow. Pricking out is done as soon as the seedlings are large enough to handle easily but before they become overcrowded. Prepare tray as for seed sowing but use a loam-based potting compost (such as John Innes No. 1) or a soilless type. Carefully lift a few seedlings with an old table

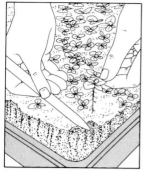

Pricking out 1

Pricking out 2

fork and separate carefully. Hold them only by the leaves. Make a hole for each one with a pencil (or a small dibber) sufficiently deep to allow roots to dangle straight down. Insert almost up to the lower leaves, then firm compost gently around the seedling, using fingers or dibber. A standard-size tray will hold about 35 seedlings, evenly spaced. Alternatively, for subjects such as greenhouse pot plants, prick off seedlings singly into 8cm/3in pots. Seedlings in peat pellets can be potted into 9cm/3½in pots before the roots start to show through the sides. Water in seedlings after pricking out, using a can with a fine rose.

■ Eight vegetative methods of propagation

Vegetative propagation involves raising plants from cuttings and by methods like layering and division.

• **Division** Used mainly for hardy perennials (herbaceous plants) but also for other clump-forming plants (for example, many alpines). The method is to split a complete clump into a number of smaller pieces, complete with roots and top growth or buds. Do this while plants are dormant, in autumn or early spring. Usually the centre portion of a clump is discarded, as it's the oldest part and declining in vigour. The young vigorous outer parts are retained for replanting. With most herbaceous plants, division for replanting should be of a size which fits into the palm of your hand. Before dividing a clump shake off most of the soil from around the roots. You can split large tough clumps with an axe. The two divisions can be split further in the same way.

• **Layering** An easy and reliable method of propagating shrubs. Especially useful for shrubs that are difficult to propagate from cuttings, such as magnolias, rhododendrons, azaleas, camellias and witch hazels. The method involves rooting a young shoot into the soil while it is still attached to the parent plant. First, you cut a 5cm/2in long "tongue" in the shoot halfway through the stem about 20–30cm/8–12in from its tip. Keep the tongue open with a small piece of wood, and peg the wounded part of the stem into a 15cm/6in deep hole in the soil, using a narrow V-shaped wire peg. Cover this part with soil. Hold the exposed tip upright by tying to a short cane. Keep well watered and within 12 months the layer should have rooted; it can then be cut away from its parent.

• **Air layering** A good way to propagate trees and shrubs. Performed in spring or summer. Use a young shoot, and about 30cm/12in from its tip cut a 5cm/2in long "tongue" halfway through its stem – as for layering. Dust the tongue with hormone rooting powder, pack it with moist sphagnum moss to hold it open, then wrap this part of the shoot with more moss, holding it in place with a "bandage" of clear polythene sheeting, sealing it at each end with waterproof adhesive tape. Within about 12 months white roots should be visible through the polythene; you can then remove it and cut the shoot from the parent plant just beyond the new roots. Some greenhouse or house plants can also be air-layered – use shoots growing about 30cm/12in from the top of the plant.

• **Root cuttings** Many shrubs and hardy perennials can be propagated from sections of young roots in the dormant season

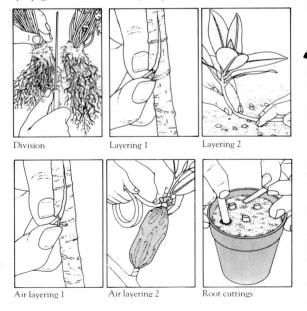

Division   Layering 1   Layering 2

Air layering 1   Air layering 2   Root cuttings (autumn/winter). Choose roots of about pencil thickness and cut into 5cm/2in lengths, making a slanting cut at the base and a flat cut at the top (to differentiate tops from bottoms when inserting). The top of the root cutting is always the part that was nearest the stem. Some plants, such as border phlox, have only very thin roots; don't worry about tops and bottoms with these. Thick root cuttings are inserted vertically to their complete length in pots or trays of cutting compost. Thin roots are laid horizontally on the surface of compost and covered with 1.25cm/½in of compost. Place in a cold frame or cold to cool greenhouse. The cutting should have rooted by the following spring or summer.

• **Leaf cuttings** This method is most applicable to greenhouse and house plants. They need warmth to root. With some subjects whole leaves are used; with others the leaves are cut up. Whole Leaves – eg African violet (*Saintpaulia*). Remove an entire leaf complete with stalk, dip in hormone rooting powder and insert several in a pot of cutting compost, to base of leaf blade. With some plants (such as *Rex begonia*), use a whole leaf but remove stalk. Turn leaf upside down, cut through main veins in several places, then place flat (the right way up) on the surface of cutting compost. Weight down with a few small stones. Plantlets eventually appear where the veins were cut through. Cut Leaves – eg mother-in-law's tongue (*Sansevieria*) and Cape primrose (*Streptocarpus*). Cut leaves into 5cm/2in long sections, dip in hormone rooting powder and insert vertically to half their length in cutting compost. It is essential to make sure they are the right way up: the edge nearest the bottom of the leaf must be placed in the compost.

• **Softwood cuttings** Many shrubs, perennials and alpines can be propagated from softwood cuttings taken in spring. Greenhouse plants, too, can be raised by this method, including fuchsias. Use soft young shoots and make the cuttings 6–8cm/2–3in long. Usually you prepare them by cutting the base immediately below a leaf joint. With some plants, such as fuchsias, you can make the bottom cut between leaf joints. Strip the leaves from the lower half of each cutting, dip bases in hormone rooting powder and insert in pots of cutting compost. Softwood cuttings need warmth and humidity to develop roots, so are best placed in a propagating case; the process normally takes only a few weeks.

• **Hardwood cuttings** Many shrubs, trees, climbers and fruits can be propagated from hardwood cuttings taken in the autumn after leaf-fall. Use current year's shoots which are well ripened – in other words, hard and woody. Cut them into 15–20cm/6–8in lengths, using secateurs. Make the top cut just above a dormant bud, and the bottom cut just below a bud. With gooseberries and redcurrants cut out all buds except the top 3 or 4. Dip bases in hormone rooting powder and insert cuttings to half to two-thirds of their length. Stand them in a V-shaped trench, return soil around them and firm it well. Many hardwoods are rooted in the open ground, but others are best placed in a cold frame. Rooting takes about a year, so lift in the following autumn.

• **Semi-ripe cuttings** Many shrubs (including evergreens), conifers and heathers can be propagated by this method in summer or autumn; you root the cuttings in heat, or in a cold frame or unheated/cool greenhouse. Use current year's side shoots which are ripe (firm and woody) at the base but still soft or unripened at the top. Average length of cuttings should be 10–15cm/4–6in. Normally you prepare them by cutting the base immediately below a leaf joint; or, if the shoots are not too long, you can pull them off the plant with a "heel" of wood attached, which you then trim clean with a knife. Strip the leaves from lower half of each cutting, dip base in hormone rooting powder and insert in containers of cutting compost. Some subjects will not be well rooted until the following year; others, such as heather root in a matter of weeks. (Heather cuttings, pulled off with a heel, should be 5cm/2in long).

■ Ten subjects to propagate by division

D ivision is a simple and reliable technique, very suitable for beginners. It improves the appearance of the parent plant and readily produces viable new plants.

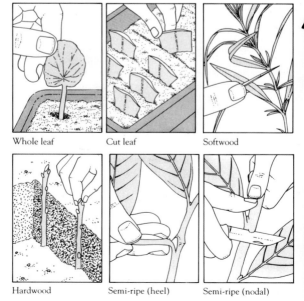

Whole leaf   Cut leaf   Softwood

Hardwood   Semi-ripe (heel)   Semi-ripe (nodal)

- **Aubrieta** Pull mats apart into small pieces during autumn.

- **Bellflower** (*Campanula*) The border kinds are vigorous and need dividing every 3 years.

- **Chrysanthemum** Hardy chrysanthemums can be split into small single shoots in spring, each with roots.

- **Golden rod** (*Solidago*) Very vigorous border plant which should be divided every 3 years.

- **Houseleek** (*Sempervivum*) Tease away rooted offsets and plant in groups.

- **Iris** German or flag irises are divided immediately after flowering in early summer. Each division consists of a portion of rhizome with a fan of leaves attached.

- **Michaelmas daisy** (*Aster*) Can be divided annually, separating the crown into single shoots with roots attached. Replant 5cm/2in apart in bold groups.

- **Ornamental grasses** Tough clumps may need splitting with an axe to divide them.

- **Plantain lily** (*Hosta*) Can be divided into single buds with roots attached if lots of plants are needed.

- **Sneezeweed** (*Helenium*) Divide plants every 3 years, pulling into hand-sized portions.

■ Five shrubs to propagate by layering

Virtually all shrubs can be propagated in this way. The following respond particularly well.

- **Azalea** Peg down shoots into a peaty soil. Roots form slowly, taking about 12 months.

- **Camellia** Best rooted in peaty soil. Takes about 12 months.

- **Lilac** (*Syringa*) Roots in about 6 months in sandy soil.

- **Magnolia** Takes 12 months to root. Peg into peaty soil and keep moist.

- **Rhododendron** Best rooted in peaty soil. Roots form slowly, taking at least 12 months.

■ Five subjects to propagate by air layering

The following plants cannot be propagated by normal layering, as their branches cannot be pulled down to the soil. Air layering "injures" the plant to encourage it to put forth roots and the stem is cut beneath the new roots.

- **Croton** (*Codiaeum*) Needs warmth and high humidity (greenhouse/house plant). May take about 12 months to root.

• **Rubber plant** (*Ficus*) Needs warmth and high humidity to root (greenhouse/house plant).

• **Witch hazel** (*Hamamelis*) Very difficult to propagate by other methods. Takes 12 months.

■ Eight subjects to propagate from root cuttings

This list includes both shrubs and perennials.

• **Anchusa** Roots easily in a cold frame.

• **Border phlox** Lay the thin cuttings flat and cover with 1.25cm/½in compost. Root in greenhouse or cold frame.

• **Drumstick primrose** (*Primula denticulata*) Root cuttings in a cold frame or greenhouse.

• **Mullein** (*Verbascum*) Some are short-lived, so propagate regularly, rooting in greenhouse or frame.

• **Ornamental quince** (*Chaenomeles*) Cuttings best rooted in greenhouse or cold frame.

• **Oriental poppy** (*Papaver orientale*) Very easy to propagate in a cold frame.

• **Sea holly** (*Eryngium*) Very easy to propagate in a cold frame. Roots very easily.

• **Stag's horn sumach** (*Rhus*) Cuttings best placed in a cold frame. Roots very easily.

■ Five subjects to propagate from leaf cuttings

Even the inexperienced gardener will find the following greenhouse and house plants very easy to propagate successfully, as long as growing conditions are controlled.

• **African violet** (*Saintpaulia*) Use whole leaf plus stalk. Needs plenty of warmth and high humidity. Can also be propagated by division of larger plants.

• **Begonia** (*Begonia rex*) Lay entire leaf flat on compost, after cutting through veins on underside. Needs constant warmth and high humidity to encourage root formation.

• **Cape primrose** (*Streptocarpus*) Cut the long leaves into 5cm/2in sections. Insert vertically. Needs warmth and humidity. Can also be propagated by division.

• **Mother-in-law's tongue** (*Sansevieria*) Cut the long leaves into 5cm/2in sections and insert vertically. Best in dryish air. Can also be propagated by division.

• **Pepper elders** (*Peperomia*) Use whole leaf plus stalk. Needs plenty of warmth and high humidity.

■ Six subjects to propagate from softwood cuttings

Success with this method depends upon providing the right conditions. Warmth and humidity are essential for good results in every case.

• **Alpines** Take small cuttings as soon as ready in spring. Best rooted in greenhouse.

• **Chrysanthemum** Outdoor and greenhouse kinds. Remove 5cm/2in-long cuttings from as close as possible to crown of plant. Root in greenhouse.

• **Dahlia** Start tubers into growth in heated greenhouse early in year. Take 8cm/3in-long cuttings from the tubers and root in warmth and humidity.

• **Delphinium** Remove 8cm/3in-long shoots from as close as possible to crown of plant in spring. Root in greenhouse.

• **Fuchsia** Take 5cm/2in-long cuttings of greenhouse fuchsias in spring as soon as ready. Root the cuttings in warmth and keep the atmosphere humid.

• **Lupin** (*Lupinus*). As for delphiniums.

■ Eleven subjects to propagate from hardwood cuttings

Hardwoods are the easiest of all cuttings to root. In addition to the following species, you can also propagate rambling and other strong-growing roses in this way, rooting them out of doors.

• **Blackcurrant** Root the cuttings in a sheltered spot outdoors or in a cold frame for protection.

• **Forsythia** Cuttings best rooted in a cold frame.

• **Jew's mallow** (*Kerria*) Root in a cold frame.

• **Dogwood** (*Cornus*) The shrubby dogwoods are best rooted in a cold frame.

• **Flowering currant** (*Ribes*) Roots very easily, especially in a cold frame. Can also be rooted outdoors in sheltered spot.

• **Gooseberry** Root in sheltered spot outdoors or in cold frame. Leave only top 3 or 4 buds.

• **Mock orange** (*Philadelphus*) Most successfully rooted in a cold frame.

• **Poplar** (*Populus*) Cuttings from those grown as shrubs are very easily rooted outdoors.

• **Red currant** Root outdoors or in a cold frame. Leave only the top 3 or 4 buds.

• **Weigela** Root in a cold frame.

• **Willow** (*Salix*) Cuttings from those grown as shrubs are very easily rooted outdoors.

■ Twelve subjects to propagate from semi-ripe cuttings

Semi-ripe cuttings root more easily than softwood. Mostly shrubs, the list also includes some perennials.

• **Barberry** (*Berberis*) Cuttings best taken early to mid-autumn. Root in greenhouse or cold frame.

• **Deutzia** Can be propagated mid to late summer in greenhouse or cold frame.

• **Escallonia** Propagate between mid-summer and mid-autumn in a frame or greenhouse.

• **Firethorn** (*Pyracantha*) Propagate late summer. Root cuttings in greenhouse or cold frame.

• **Forsythia** Take cuttings mid-summer and root in cold frame or greenhouse.

• **Geranium** (*Pelargonium*) Take cuttings late summer, rooting them in a greenhouse or cold frame. Dry atmosphere needed.

• **Heathers** (*Erica, Calluna*) Pull off heather cuttings with a "heel" of wood attached. Should be around 5cm/2in long. Root as soon as ready between early summer and early autumn. Rooting is quick in heat, slower in cold frame.

• **Laurel** (*Prunus*) Take cuttings early or mid-autumn and root in cold frame or outdoors.

• **Lavender** (*Lavandula*) Propagate early to mid-autumn and root in cold frame.

• **Mock orange** (*Philadelphus*) Take cuttings mid to late summer. Root in cold frame.

• **Shrubby veronica** (*Hebe*) Take cuttings mid-summer to mid-autumn. Root in greenhouse or cold frame.

• **Weigela** Take cuttings as soon as ready, between early and late summer. Root in greenhouse in warmth.

PLANTING AND PLANT CARE

Planting techniques vary slightly according to whether you buy plants in containers from garden centres or bare-root plants (as lifted from the field) supplied by nurserymen. There are also various ways of planting bulbs. Get the technique right and plant at the right time: your plants will then be off to a good start. Some plants will need supports against the wind.

■ Four planting methods

These are the techniques for planting the major groups of garden plants: trees, shrubs, conifers, climbers, perennials, bedding plants and blubs. To get plants such as trees, shrubs, conifers and fruits off to a good start, especially if you have a poor or difficult soil, consider using a planting mixture. You can buy proprietary mixtures or you can make your own – a bucketful of moist peat or coco fibre mixed with a small handful of blood, bone and fishmeal. A spadeful of planting mixture can be forked into the soil in the bottom of the planting hole, and more mixed in with the solid which is to be returned around the roots.

• **Bare-root plants** If you buy from a local or mail-order nurseryman, you may well find that the plants are not in containers or do not have a ball of soil around the roots. The roots should, however, be wrapped to prevent drying out. Deciduous shrubs, trees and climbers, as well as hardy perennials, may be supplied in this way; also tree, bush and case fruits. Bare-root plants are sold and planted in the dormant season – late autumn to early spring. The technique is simple. First take out a planting hole deep enough to allow the roots to spread out (or to dangle straight down in the case of perennials) to their full extent. Return some fine soil over the roots and gently shake the plant up and down to work the soil well between them. Firm with your heels. Then return the rest of the soil, firming as you proceed. Always plant to the same depth that the plants were growing in the nursery – indicated by a soil mark at the base of the stem or trunk. The dormant buds (crown) of perennials must not be covered with soil.

• **Bedding plants** Spring-flowering bedding plants, such as wallflowers (*Cheiranthus cheiri*) are planted in early autumn, summer-flowering ones in late spring or early summer, when danger of frost is over. Wallflowers may be bought as bare-root plants, in which case use the planting technique described above. However, most spring and summer bedding plants are supplied in containers, such as pots, trays and plastic strips. Before planting, water the plants to make sure compost is thoroughly moist. Carefully remove the plants from their containers so as not to damage or disturb the roots. In the case of bedding plants in trays, carefully tease plants apart using a hand fork, aiming to retain as much soil as possible around the roots. Take out planting holes large enough to take roots or root-balls without cramping. Return fine soil around roots and firm with your hands. Water in thoroughly if soil is dry.

• **Bulbs** Spring-flowering bulbs are planted in early autumn; summer and autumn-flowering kinds in spring or summer. Planting depths (amount of soil over tops of bulbs) varies according to size of bulb. As a guide, small or miniature bulbs such as crocuses are planted in holes 8cm/3in deep, while larger kinds such as daffodils can be planted in holes 15cm/6in deep. When planting a few bulbs you can make the holes with a hand trowel. For a lot of bulbs use a bulb planter, which takes out a core of soil; place bulb in hole and return the core. A bulb planter is useful too for planting in grass. Whichever method you use, always ensure bottom of bulb is in close contact with soil. For large drifts of bulbs in grass, you might find it easiest to lift an area of turf, plant the bulbs (with a trowel or bulb planter), then re-lay turf.

• **Container-grown plants** Plants bought from garden centres in containers can be planted any time of year, provided the soil is not frozen or excessively wet. Conifers and other evergreen shrubs are sometimes supplied with a ball of soil around the roots, which is tightly wrapped with hessian. These can also be considered as container-grown plants, but are only bought and planted in early autumn or mid-spring. The planting technique is as follows. Take out a hole only slightly larger than the root-ball. Carefully remove the plant from its container, avoiding root disturbance. Place plant in centre of hole and return fine soil around rootball, firming it thoroughly. The top of the root-ball should be only slightly below the soil surface after planting.

■ Five ways to support plants

Newly planted trees and some shrubs will be able to support themselves as soon as roots are well established but require staking initially, particularly in windy gardens. Garden plants with large heavy blooms (such as dahlias and chrysanthemums) need constant support. For climbers see p90.

• **Canes** Bamboo canes of appropriate height can be used to support thin-stemmed hardy perennials, such as Michaelmas daisies (*Aster*). Insert 3 in a triangular formation around a clump, before the stems become too high; encircle the stems as they grow with loops of green gardening string. Single canes can be used for newly planted tall shrubs such as brooms (*Cytisus*) and certain conifers, particularly Leyland cypress (× *Cupressocyparis*); tie in stems with soft green garden string. Single canes are also recommended for gladioli, delphiniums and chrysanthemums.

• **Metal plant supports** These are proprietary wire hoops on legs, useful for hardy perennials. The support encircles the stems and comes in various sizes.

• **Tree stakes** You put in a tree stake after you have dug the planting hole. Use either a length of 5 x 5cm/2 x 2in timber or a larch pole. Bury this in the hole just off-centre, to windward of where the trunk will be in its central position. Top of stake should be just below the lowest branch. With stake firmly in place, plant the tree. Then fix one tree tie 5cm/2in from top of stake and another 30cm/12in above soil level. Use proprietary plastic buckle-type ties; check regularly and loosen as necessary. Remove stake after a couple of years, once the tree is well rooted into the soil; otherwise the tree will come to rely on it and may make only a weak root system. (Some gardeners prefer to use a stake that protrudes just 30cm/12in from the soil, attached to the tree by one tie. This allows more tree movement, which is said to promote rooting).

• **Twiggy sticks** Bushy herbaceous plants (hardy perennials) and hardy annuals may be supported by pushing twiggy sticks or branches among them while they are small. As the plants grow they mask the branches but are held steady by them.

• **Wooden stakes** Dahlias, standard roses and other top-heavy plants may be supported with 2.5cm/1in square wooden stakes pushed into the ground alongside them. Fasten stems to supports with soft twine – or strong tarred twine for standard roses which are permanently staked.

PRUNING

A mystique surrounds pruning – a shroud of confusion which few gardening books and journals succeed in penetrating. As a result, many gardeners prune incorrectly or indiscriminately. It is wrong to think that all shrubs need a "good haircut" every year. The truth is, most shrubs do not need any pruning; all you need to do is look over them occasionally and if necessary cut out any dead or dying shoots or branches. Conifers need pruning only when grown as ornamental hedges; ornamental trees do not need pruning at all; most climbers are happier if left alone, and so are most roses – although some, such as bush roses, need severe pruning every year.

For fruit trees and bushes (which require regular pruning each year) the procedure can be quite complex, depending on the forms or shapes you wish to grow; it is advisable to consult a specialist fruit book. Pruning of bush and cane fruits is more straightforward, and some hints are given on pp126-7.

■ Five reasons for pruning

Y ou should not prune shrubs, climbers and so on unless there is a specific reason. Pruning must benefit the plant in some way – for example to improve shape or flowering, or both. There are five main reasons for pruning.

• **To remove dead wood** Check over all shrubs, trees, conifers, climbers and roses regularly – once or twice a year – and if you see any dead stems or shoots cut them out, or cut back to live tissue. Dead material, of course, is more easily spotted when plants are in leaf.

• **To improve flowering** Some plants produce more and bet-ter-quality flowers if you prune them regularly each year. To ensure that flowers are produced on young wood, remove old flowered wood – with some shrubs immediately after flower-ing, with others in late winter or early spring. Bush roses espe-cially need pruning to produce plenty of healthy young wood.

• **To improve fruiting** With tree, bush and cane fruits you must prune to promote the growth of fruit-bearing wood. Tree fruits such as apples and pears produce fruits on short fruiting "spurs" on the main branches. Bush and cane fruits produce crops on young, previous year's shoots.

• **To control shape** Pruning to encourage a definite shape is a method applied mainly to fruit tree forms: for example, cor-dons, espaliers, fans and dwarf bush trees (see pp59–60). Formal hedges are also pruned to a definite shape, such as a wedge form. Shrubs are pruned so that their natural shape is retained, while bush roses are encouraged to form an open centre, rather like a vase. Climbers are "shaped" more by train-ing than by pruning.

• **To control size** Many forms of pruning restrict the size of plants. This applies especially to hedges, and also to trained fruit trees. Hard pruning of flowering shrubs and roses will limit the plants' dimensions. Judicious cutting back of climbers will prevent them from becoming too tall or spreading too far.

■ **Four pruning methods for garden shrubs**

The habit of an ornamental shrub determines the pruning method employed. Examples of all four groups below are given on pp55–7.

• **Group 1:** deciduous shrubs that flower on shoots produced during previous growing season. The flowers are formed either on short laterals produced from this 1-year-old-wood, or directly from the 1-year-old-branches. Many spring- and early summer-flowering shrubs belong to this group. Immediately after flowering cut back branches or stems that have borne flowers to young shoots growing lower down: these young shoots will flower the following year. At the same time remove completely about one-quarter of the oldest stems.

• **Group 2:** deciduous shrubs that bear flowers on current year's growth. When pruned hard back in late winter/early spring these shrubs produce vigorous shoots which flower in summer or early autumn. Pruning may consist of simply cut-ting out all growth to ground level (for small sub-shrubby plants such as hardy fuchsias); or allowing a framework of woody branches to develop to the required height and then cutting back the growths close to this framework, to within one or two buds (as with *Buddleia davidii*).

• **Group 3:** deciduous shrubs pruned in early spring each year to obtain maximum decorative effect from their bark in winter. Examples are shrubby dogwoods (*Cornus alba*) and willows (*Salix*). Techniques similar to that for Group 2: on framework of older stems of various heights, prune shoots hard back, to within a bud or two of their base.

• **Group 4:** evergreen and deciduous shrubs that need their dead flowers removed immediately after flowering, mainly to prevent seed production and so encourage stronger growth.

Group 1

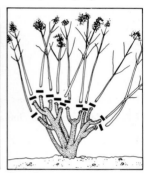

Group 2

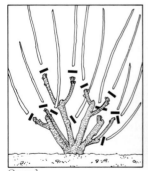

Group 3

Group 4

■ Thirteen subjects to prune in late winter or spring

These are popular deciduous shrubs, climbers and roses, all of which flower even better if regularly pruned.

• **Butterfly bush** (*Buddleia davidii*) Group 2. Allow a frame-work of woody branches to required height.

• **Californian lilac** (*Ceanothus*) Group 2 (deciduous ceanothus only). Allow a framework of woody branches to form, and cut back to keep it at the required height.

• **Clematis** Pruning technique for these climbers varies according to type. See p57 for detailed advice.

• **Dogwood** (*Cornus alba* and varieties, *Cornus stolonifera* 'Flaviramea') Shrubby dogwoods with coloured winter bark. The young bark has the best colour. Group 3.

• **Flowering currant** (*Ribes sanguineum*) Group 1. Prune in spring, after the plant has flowered.

• **Forsythia** Group 1. Prune in spring.

• **Fuchsia** Hardy fuchsias are in Group 2. Cut out all growth to ground level.

• **Hydrangea** (*Hydrangea macrophylla*) Group 1. Although these bloom in summer, prune in late winter – lightly cut back old flowered stems, especially if killed back by frost. Remove some of oldest wood.

• **Jew's mallow** (*Kerria japonica*) Group 1. Prune in spring.

• **Roses, bush types and climbers**. See p58.

• **Spiraea** (*Spiraea* x *Arguta* and *S. thunbergii*) Group 1. Prune in spring/early summer.

• **Willow** (*Salix*) Willows grown as shrubs for coloured winter bark come into Group 3.

• **Winter jasmine** (*Jasminum nudiflorum*) This popular climber is in Group 2. Prune in early spring.

■ **Six subjects to prune in summer or autumn**

These include various summer-flowering shrubs, climbers and formal hedges. (The groups are defined on pp54–5.)

• **Deutzia** Group 1. Prune in early summer.

• **Hedges** Formal hedges are pruned in summer. Small-leaved kinds such as privet (*Ligustrum ovalifolium*) can be trimmed with shears or an electric trimmer; large-leaved kinds such as laurel should be trimmed with secateurs. Some hedges need more trimming than others to keep them looking neat: examples are privet and Chinese honeysuckle (*Lonicera nitida*), both fast growers (privet may need trimming 4 or 5 times). Other hedging plants need clipping only once a year, usually late summer. See pp13–15.

• **Mock orange** (*Philadelphus* varieties) Group 1. Prune in summer, after the plant has flowered.

• **Rose, ramblers**. See p58.

• **Weigela** Group 1. Prune in summer.

• **Wisteria** Train to make a framework of permanent stems. These produce side shoots which bear flowers in spring/early summer. In late summer cut back the side shoots to about 15cm/6in from their base as they become very long. Further shorten these flowering "spurs" in winter, leaving only 2 or 3 buds on each.

■ Six popular plants that need dead heading

These evergreen and deciduous shrubs fall into Group 4 (see p55): they need to have dead blooms removed immediately after flowering.

• **Broom** (*Cytisus*) Using secateurs, cut off tops of shoots containing developing seed pods. On no account cut into older wood when pruning broom.

• **Heather** (*Calluna, Erica*) Lightly trim over plants with shears to remove dead heads. Do not cut into older wood.

• **Lavender** (*Lavandula*) Trim off dead flowers with shears, including the long stalks.

• **Lilac** (*Syringa*) Cut off dead blooms with secateurs. Take care not to damage new buds immediately below.

• **Rhododendron** You can easily twist off dead flower heads, but avoid damaging new buds immediately below.

• **Shrubby cinquefoil** (*Potentilla fruticosa* varieties) Lightly trim over with shears after flowering. This helps to keep plants dense and bushy.

■ Three pruning methods for clematis

Large vigorous species (such as the very popular *Clematis montana*) can be grown through trees and left unpruned, but in most other situations most clematis will before long become a tangled mass of growth unless you prune them. Clematis are of several types and can be grouped according to pruning needs as follows.

• **Group 1:** all clematis species and hybrids that flower in summer and autumn entirely on new growths produced during current season. Cut back whole of previous year's growth virtually to ground level in late winter. Cut immediately above strong buds. Examples: *C. orientalis, C. tangutica, C. viticella, C.* x *jackmanii*, 'Ernest Markham', 'Hagley Hybrid', 'Perle d'Azur', 'Graveye Beauty', 'Etoile Rose'.

• **Group 2:** mainly vigorous spring-flowering species which bloom on short shoots from growth produced the previous summer. Examples: *C. montana* and varieties, *C. alpina* and *C. macropetala*. The first is very vigorous and is best given ample space and left unpruned, although it can be cut back to keep it within bounds. Others are pruned by cutting away all flowered wood to within a few centimetres/inches of main framework immediately after flowering (spring or early summer).

• **Group 3:** all the hybrids that provide large flowers from late spring to mid-summer on previous year's wood. Examples: 'Lasurstern', 'Nelly Moser', 'The President', 'Henryi', 'Vyvyan Pennell', 'William Kennett', 'Duchess of Edinburgh'. Clematis in this group may be left unpruned or only lightly pruned until they become straggly or out of control, when they can be cut back to within about 90cm/3ft of ground level in late winter. Alternatively you can treat them as Group 1 and prune them back hard to base in late winter; then they will flower only in late summer.

■ Three pruning methods for roses

P runing roses will not reward you with more flowers next year. However, it will control shape and maintain health. Wild (species) roses and hybrid shrub roses need no pruning – just the removal of dead wood.

• **Bush types** Large-flowered (hybrid tea) and cluster-flowered (floribunda) roses are pruned annually in early spring. Remove all weak growth and reduce remaining strong stems to 15–20cm/6–8in above ground level. Cut to outward-facing buds. Make sure centre of each bush is free from growth: shape bush like a vase.

• **Climbers** Allow a framework of permanent stems which are trained to their supports. From these stems side shoots grow, which produce the flowers. To prune, cut back old side shoots to within one or two buds of their base in early spring. Tips of main stems can also be cut back, if becoming too tall.

• **Ramblers** These roses produce new stems from ground level, which flower the following year. Prune immediately after flowering in early autumn. Cut out completely the old flowered stems and train the new ones in their place.

■ Nine popular shrubs you need not prune

T hese plants only need to have dead wood cut out as necessary. With deciduous shrubs this is most easily done when they are in leaf.

• **Barberries** (*Berberis*) Deciduous and evergreen shrubs noted for flowers and/or berries.

• **Camellia** Handsome evergreens with winter or spring flowers. Only for lime-free soil.

• **Cotoneaster** Deciduous and evergreen shrubs noted for autumn berries.

• **Elaeagnus** Evergreen kinds with gold-splashed leaves are highly recommended for winter effect.

• **Escallonia** Evergreens with pink, red or white summer flowers. Ideal for coastal gardens.

• **Firethorn** (*Pyracantha*) Evergreen with heavy crops of autumn berries.

• **Magnolia** Only dead branches or those that get in the way should be cut out in summer.

• **Viburnum** Evergreen and deciduous shrubs grown for their flowers and/or berries.

• **Witch hazel** (*Hamamelis*) Among the most attractive winter-flowering shrubs. Best in a slightly acid to neutral soil.

∎ Six fruit tree forms

The first five types described below are ideal for small gardens or where space is limited. Pruning techniques are quite complex and should be studied in a specialist fruit book.

• **Cordon** A single straight stem is furnished with side-shoots or fruit spur kept short by summer pruning and sometimes by winter pruning. Cordons are planted in a line and the stems are sloped at 45°, as shown in the diagram below. The trees are spaced about 75cm/2½in apart and are supported with a system of 1.8m/6ft high posts and horizontal wires, plus a supporting cane for each. Suitable for apples, pears, white currants, gooseberries.

• **Dwarf bush** Suitable for apples, pears, plums, peaches and morello cherries. These trees are grown on dwarfing rootstocks to keep them small. The trunk is usually only about 60cm/2ft high, and branches radiate from it. The centre of the tree is kept open (free from branches) so that it resembles an inverted open umbrella in shape.

• **Dwarf pyramid** Suitable for apples, pears, plums and cherries. A kind of free-growing vertical cordon, but easier to prune. Dwarfing rootstocks are used. The branches from the central stem are pruned to a pyramid shape.

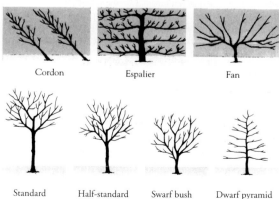

Cordon   Espalier   Fan

Standard   Half-standard   Swarf bush   Dwarf pyramid

• **Espalier** An alternative method for apples and pears. From a central stem, horizontal fruiting "arms" (tiers) grow at about 38–45cm/15–18in intervals. The tree is trained in one plane – for example, against a wall or fence. Fruits are borne on spurs on the fruiting arms, which are pruned in summer. Space the espaliers 3–4.5m/10–12ft apart in a line, and support them with a 1.8m/6ft high system of posts and wires.

• **Fan** Suitable for plums, cherries and peaches. A perfectly flat tree, often trained against a wall or fence. From the top of a very short trunk branches radiate in a fan shape; these produce lateral shoots which bear the fruits.

• **Standard** Suitable for apples, pears, plums and other top fruits. The tall stem supports a well-spaced head of branches. Not for small gardens. A half-standard has a shorter main stem than a standard, although not as short as a bush.

GROWING UNDER GLASS

If money is no object you can now have a greenhouse or conservatory that looks after itself, with the plants watered automatically. On a more modest scale, garden frames and cloches are extremely useful (and comparatively inexpensive) pieces of equipment: they are of particular value on the vegetable plot for extending the growing season at either end.
Eight types of greenhouse

Today greenhouses come in all shapes and sizes to suit every need and site.

• **Span-roof greenhouse** The traditional greenhouse, with pitched roof (each side of equal size and shape) sloping down to the eaves. Normally has straight sides, although there are models with sloping sides which result in better light penetration. The glass-to-ground types are ideal for growing plants at ground level, such as tomatoes in growing-bags; those with solid sides (to about 90cm/3ft) are good for pot plants, as they retain heat better than all-glass houses. Framework available in aluminium alloy or timber (such as western red cedar). You can now obtain span-roof greenhouses with curved eaves.

• **Lean-to greenhouse** Greenhouse built against a wall, resembling half of a span-roof greenhouse (see above). Has a lighter framework than a conservatory. Available in aluminium or timber. May be glazed to the ground or have solid sides to a height of about 90cm/3ft.

• **Mansard greenhouse** Also known as a curvilinear greenhouse. The roof panels are set at various angles, giving a curved shape to the roof and ensuring excellent light intensity inside. Glass-to-ground, or solid walls to about 90cm/3ft. Aluminum framework. Lean-to versions also available.

• **Round greenhouse** Free-standing structure with 6, 9 or 12 sides – actually lantern-shaped, not truly round. Looks attractive in an ornamental setting, such as a large patio. Timber or aluminum framework; glass-to-ground or half-timber sides.

• **Mini greenhouse** Both free-standing and lean-to types are marketed. Ideal for patios and balconies. Access is by sliding or hinged doors, although a true mini is too small to step inside. Will hold a growing bag for tomatoes; also useful for plant raising. Aluminium or timber framework, usually glazed to ground. Can heat up excessively in warm weather unless you pay careful attention to ventilation.

• **Dome-shaped greenhouse** Also known as the geodesic greenhouse, this is virtually a glass dome with an aluminium framework. Very light and roomy inside. Available in various sizes. Looks superb in a modern setting and highly recommended for ornamental plant displays.

• **Conservatory** Built against a wall of the house – ideally a warm sunny wall. Types vary from a simple lean-to style greenhouse (the structure is heavier than a true lean-to) to a more elaborate nineteenth-century style building. Ideally designed as an integral part of the house with access from one of the rooms. Often the building has solid sides to a height of about 90cm/3ft, although models are available with glass to the ground. Conservatories are available as modular systems supplied in sections of timber construction. There are also less expensive kits with a framework of aluminium alloy.

• **Polythene tunnel** Comparatively cheap structure, ideal for growing vegetables and raising plants, provided that they don't require very warm conditions – tunnels are not well insulated, so would be quite costly to heat. Framework consists of galvanized tubular-steel hoops inserted in ground and covered with flexible polythene "skin". A door at each end provides access and ventilation. The polythene will need replacing every 3 years or so, as it becomes brittle and discoloured.

■ Two types of greenhouse staging

Staging is recommended if you want to grow pot plants and is also convenient for raising plants. It allows maximum use of greenhouse space, especially if arranged in two or more tiers. Tiered staging is particularly useful for lean-to greenhouses and conservatories, as it can be placed against the back wall to create an attractive massed display.

• **Aluminium** A tubular-aluminium staging framework is the sensible choice for an aluminium-framed greenhouse or conservatory. Some systems are easily dismantled so that you can move out the staging for the summer to accommodate tall crops such as tomatoes. Many systems are extendable.

• **Timber** Looks best in a greenhouse or conservatory with a timber structure. Available in cedarwood or deal, single-level or tiered. Not so versatile as aluminium staging – generally considered a permanent fixture.

■ Two types of staging surface

Plant pots can stand on one of two types of surface. Choose the surface to suit the plants you intend to grow.

• **Slatted or open-work surface** Recommended for pot plants and orchids, which like good air circulation. Also allows surplus water to drain quickly and heat to rise around the plants. There is a choice of timber slats or plastic openwork units.

• **Gravel trays** Designed to hold gravel, shingle or horticultural aggregate. If these materials are kept moist a humid atmosphere is created around the plants. This is appreciated by many pot plants, especially tropical and sub-tropical kinds. Gravel trays can also be used for capillary watering if filled with sand or lined with capillary matting (see p63).

■ Four ways to heat a greenhouse

A common mistake is to buy a heater too small for the greenhouse so that the desired minimum temperature is unobtainable during really cold weather. Seek the heater manufacturer's advice on the size of the unit, quoting the dimensions of your greenhouse and the desired minimum temperature. As a general guide, the following examples are instructive. To maintain a 2.4 x 1.8m/8 x 6ft greenhouse at 5°C/40°F when the outside temperature is -7°C/20°F, you will need a heater with an output of 2kw/6,000 BTUs. To maintain a minimum of 10°C/50°F in the same greenhouse you will need a heater with an output of 3kw/9,000 BTUs. A heated greenhouse should be insulated to keep fuel bills at a realistic level. The most popular method is to line the inside of the greenhouse with bubble plastic insulation (sold specifically for greenhouse use). This can be taken down in summer when the heater is switched off.

• **Electric heater** Electricity is efficient, reliable, automatic, convenient and clean. It's also quite expensive compared with other fuels, although thermostatic control (considered essential) will keep down costs. The most popular type of electric greenhouse heater is the fan heater, which blows out warm air. Tubular heaters are hollow tubes containing heating elements; they are generally installed in "banks" along the sides of the greenhouse or under the staging. Neat and compact.

• **Gas heater** Basically a warm-air cabinet: air is warmed inside and rises out of the top. Natural-gas types are cheaper to run than bottled-gas models. Both are thermostatically controlled. Minimum attention.

• **Paraffin heater** Portable and highly popular but it needs frequent attention (regular filling and cleaning). Some ventilation must be provided at all times. Often thought to be cheaper to run than other types of heater but not thermostatic – so can be more expensive. Two types available: blue-flame models, with less risk of fumes (these are harmful to plants); and yellow-flame models, which are almost as good. Always use high-grade paraffin.

• **Soil-warming cables** Electric warming cables laid underneath a soil bed or in a sand bed on the greenhouse staging. They provide bottom heat, which is especially useful for propagation. Cheap to run, especially with thermostatic control. They do not heat the air, so a greenhouse heater will be needed to maintain air temperatures.

■ Three ways to ventilate and shade a greenhouse

Very hot sun can severely scorch or damage plants under glass, so some form of shading is needed between mid-spring and early autumn. A greenhouse must also be well ventilated to prevent a damp, stuffy, stagnant atmosphere and to keep temperatures down in hot weather.

• **Automatic ventilator openers** All ventilators can be fitted with automatic ventilator arms, which open and close them according to temperature. These are reasonably priced; no power source is needed.

• **External blinds** To provide shade you can fit roller blinds to the outside of the greenhouse. Most are manually operated but there are automatic systems (expensive, naturally!). Available in various materials, including wooden laths, plastic reeds and shading netting.

• **Liquid shading materials** Proprietary products which are "painted" on to the outside of the glass to provide shade. Apply in spring and wash off in early autumn.

■ Two automatic watering systems

If you cannot regularly attend to watering, consider an automatic system which runs from a header tank connected to the mains water supply (or a semi-automatic system which is supplied by a reservoir).

• **Capillary watering** Pots are placed on water-retentive capillary matting and take up moisture as required. The matting can be laid in gravel trays. Complete watering systems are available, with trays, matting and sometimes water reservoirs.

• **Trickle watering** Popularly known as the "spaghetti system": a main plastic supply pipe with thin tubes sprouting from it. Each tube is positioned over a pot or container so every plant is watered when the supply is turned on.

■ Three composts for pot plants

Use a good proprietary compost for greenhouse plants – not ordinary garden soil.

• **Loam-based composts (such as John Innes)** These consist of loam, peat and sand, plus fertilizer and chalk. J.I. seed compost should be used for seed sowing. There are three grades of potting compost: No. 1, which is used for pricking off seedlings and potting rooted cuttings; No. 2, formulated for potting young plants on into larger pots; and No. 3, which is a very rich compost, to be used only for very large plants and for final potting of greenhouse chrysanthemums.

• **Proprietary soilless composts** These usually consist entirely of peat, with fertilizers added. Very clean and light in weight. Seed and potting composts are available. Don't firm them too much, and avoid overwatering.

• **Specialist composts** For growing spring-flowering bulbs in bowls (hyacinths, daffodils, tulips) use bulb fibre, which consists mainly of peat. There are special composts available for cacti and succulents. If potting lime-hating plants, such as azaleas and camellias, use an ericaceous compost (one which does not contain lime or chalk).

■ Four types of cloche

Cloches are low structures generally used on the vegetable plot to cover rows of vegetables, especially early and late sowing. Formerly always made of glass, they are now available in polythene and plastic. They help to warm the soil and protect plants from the elements, thus enabling you to extend the growing season.

• **Barn cloche** Four glass or clear-plastic sheets held together with special wire clips. The shape resembles a span-roof greenhouse. The barn cloche has plenty of headroom. Several are placed end to end to form a continuous "run" along a row of crops. Close the ends with sheets of glass or rigid plastic.

• **Low polythene tunnel** Bought in kit form. Consists of a long sheet of clear or white polythene stretched over galvanized-wire hoops. The edges of the polythene are buried in the soil. A comparatively cheap form of cloche which can last for several years if you are careful.

• **Tent** Two sheets of glass or rigid clear plastic held together with special clips, to form a tent shape. These cloches are placed end to end, as with barn cloches, to form a sheltered tunnel, but they do not have so much headroom. Ideal for small crops such as lettuces.

• **Corrugated plastic sheeting** Can be bent over rows of crops and anchored with wire hoops.

■ Three types of garden frame

A garden frame, also known as a cold frame, is a low struc-ture which provides protection for plants. In it you can raise many plants from seeds or cuttings, you can grow early crops of small vegetables such as lettuces and carrots, or you can harden off plants raised in a heated greenhouse, prior to planting them out in the garden.

• **Double-span** Shaped like a low span-roof greenhouse. Typically 45–60cm/1½–2ft high at the ridge, sloping to 23–30cm/9–12in at the sides. Framework may be aluminium or timber. Sides may be solid or glass. Top glass covers either slide or lift for access.

• **Dutch lights** Useful if you want to make your own garden frame. The frame sides and ends could be constructed of tim-ber or brickwork; then Dutch lights are placed on top. You can have double-span or single-span frames – depending on your DIY skills. Each Dutch light consists of a simple timber frame-work holding a large pane of horticultural glass. Size is 1.5 x 0.75m/5 x 2½ft. You may have to search for a supplier.

• **Single-span** Rather like a low lean-to greenhouse – designed to be placed against a wall. Typically 45–60cm/1½–2ft high at the back, sloping to 23–30cm/9–12in at the front. Available in timber or aluminium, with solid or glass sides and ends.

PLANTS FOR EVERY PURPOSE

ANNUALS AND BIENNIALS

Annuals and biennials flower once before dying. They are easily raised from seeds and are thus a compara-tively inexpensive – but time-consuming – way to pro-vide a wealth of colour in spring or summer, whether for container gardening, for bedding schemes, as a plentiful source of cut flowers, or as colourful fillers in a border or rock garden. Most plants in both cate-gories perform best when situated in plenty of sun and planted in well-drained soil.

Hardy annuals are sown outdoors in early to mid-spring in the place where they are to flower. Half-hardy annuals (also known as summer bedding plants) are frost-tender and need to be raised in a green-house in early or mid-spring and planted out when the danger of frost is over. Some hardy annuals propagate themselves by self-sowing.

Biennials include spring bedding plants and sum-mer-flowering border plants. They are sown outdoors in late spring, transferred to their flowering positions in autumn, and bloom the following year.

■ **Fourteen annuals and biennials for the mixed border**

For growing around and among shrubs and herbaceous plants, it is best to choose annuals that are not gaudy. The following will harmonize well with the permanent border plants, rather than compete for attention.

• **Baby blue eyes** (*Nemophila menziesii*) Hardy annual with saucer-shaped white-eyed blue flowers in summer. 20cm/8in high. Likes moist soil and succeeds in sun or dappled shade.

• **Blazing star** (*Mentzelia lindleyi*) Hardy annual with scented yellow flowers all summer. 45cm/18in. A good choice for sandy soil in a sunny spot.

• **Californian poppy** (*Eschscholzia californica*).Hardy annual with yellow, orange, pink or red flowers in summer. 40cm/16in. Flowers best in poor light soil with plenty of sun.

• **Californian bluebell** (*Phacelia campanularia*) Hardy blue-flowered annual, 25cm/10in, for sun and sandy soil.

• **Canary creeper** (*Tropaeolum peregrinum*) Hardy annual climber growing to 3.6m/12ft. Yellow flowers in summer. Grow plants up a wigwam of tall bamboo canes or, even better, allow them to scramble over large shrubs.

• **Canterbury bells** (*Campanula medium*) Hardy biennial with spikes of bell-like flowers in several colours, early summer. Grows up to 90cm/3ft, although 'Bells of Holland' is half this height. Tolerates dappled shade.

• **Foxglove** (*Digitalis purpurea*) Hardy biennial with spikes of tubular flowers in early summer. Tallest is the 'Excelsior' strain (1.5m/5ft); large spikes in many colours. Grows well in dry soil and dappled shade.

• **Honesty** (*Lunaria annua*) Hardy biennial with purple flowers in spring, followed by silvery seed pods which are excellent for cutting and drying. Grows anywhere, to 60cm/2ft.

• **Love-lies-bleeding** (*Amaranthus caudatus*) A half-hardy annual with red tassel-like flowers in summer. Up to 90cm/3ft. Takes poor soil in its stride, but likes sun.

• **Snow-on-the-mountain** (*Euphorbia marginata*) Hardy annual with white-edged leaves (the flowers are hardly noticeable). Colour best if soil poor and dry. 60cm/2ft.

• **Spider flower** (*Cleome spinosa*) Half-hardy annual with large, scented, spidery pink blooms in summer; grows to 1.2m/4ft. A sun-worshipper, for rich soil.

• **Sweet William** (*Dianthus barbatus*) A favourite old cottage-garden hardy biennial with early summer flowers in many colours. 30–60cm/1–2ft. Grows well in chalky soils.

• **Tobacco plant** (*Nicotiana alata*) Popular cottage-garden plant whose flowers in many colours are valued for their scent. Half-hardy annual, summer flowering. 30–90cm/1–3ft. Likes rich soil and sun.

• **Vervain** (*Verbena x hybrida*) Half-hardy bushy annual with a ground-covering habit. 15–45cm/6–18in high. Clusters of flowers in many colours all summer. Likes good soil and sun.

■ Sixteen annuals for cutting

To extend the lift of a cut flower display, pick the blooms in the early morning or in the evening. Cut at an angle to expose more water-carrying cells. The following are specially recommended for cutting, as the flowers are long-lasting when arranged in water.

• **Chalk plant** (*Gypsophila elegans*) Half-hardy annual with sprays of tiny white flowers in summer. 45–60cm/1½–2ft. A good choice for chalky soils.

• **China aster** (*Callistephus chinensis*) Half-hardy annual. Blooms (mid-summer to autumn) vary from chrysanthemum shape to pompon, and come in many colours. 30–60cm/1–2ft. Sun and good soil are needed for best results; but choose a sheltered spot for tall varieties.

• **Chrysanthemum (annual)** (*Chrysanthemum carinatum*) Hardy annual with brilliant multicoloured daisy flowers in summer. 45–60cm/1½–2ft. Likes fertile soil and sun. Provide twiggy sticks for support. Remove initial flower beds to encourage longer flower stems.

• **Coneflower** (*Rudbeckia hirta*) Half-hardy annual with large gold or mahogany daisy flowers in summer. 30–90cm/1–3ft. Full sun, twiggy sticks for support. Cut back after first flush of blooms to ensure more follow.

• **Cornflower** (*Centaurea cyanus*) Hardy annual with, typically, blue frilly flowers in summer. 30–90cm/1–3ft. Needs sun, good soil and twiggy sticks for support.

• **Cosmos** (*Cosmos bipinnatus*) Half-hardy annual with long succession of pink, red or white flowers from summer until the arrival of the first frosts. 0.9–1.2m/3–4ft. Ideal for a hot dry spot with poor soil.

• **Gaillardia** (*Gaillardia pulchella*) Hardy annual, double daisy flowers in many colours through summer into autumn. 45–60cm/1½–2ft. Good on sandy soil in full sun.

• **Godetia** (*Godetia grandiflora*) Hardy compact annual with single or double azalea-like blooms in pink, red, purple, etc, all summer. 30–60cm/1–2ft. Likes moist soil – but not too rich, or blooms will be few.

• **Larkspur** (*Delphinium consolida*) A hardy, branching annual with bold spikes of flowers in many colours throughout summer. 0.9–1.2m/3–4ft. Needs sun and shelter, and support of twiggy sticks.

• **Love-in-a-mist** (*Nigella damascena*) Hardy annual with feathery leaves and summer flowers in blue or mixed colours. 45–60cm/1½–2ft. The inflated seed pods which follow can be dried for winter display. Likes plenty of sun.

• **Pot marigold** (*Calendula officinalis*) Popular and easy hardy annual with pungent foliage and orange or yellow daisy flowers in summer and autumn. 30–60cm/1–2ft. Good for poor soils. Can self-sow.

• **Scabious** (*Scabiosa atropurpurea*) Hardy annual with soft blue pincushion blooms, also available in various colours, flowering summer and autumn. 45–90cm/1½–3ft. Needs good soil, sun and supports for stems.

• **Statice** (*Limonium sinuatum*) Hardy annual with clusters of flowers in many colours, summer and early autumn. 45cm/1½ft. The blooms are usually dried for winter decoration – hang them upside down, in bunches, in a cool, dry airy place for a few weeks. Needs full sun.

• **Strawflower** (*Helichrysum bracteatum*) Half-hardy annual with papery daisy flowers in many bright colours in summer, suitable for drying (see Statice). 30–90cm/1–3ft. Sandy soil, plenty of sun (poor flower colour in rich soils).

• **Sweet pea** (*Lathyrus odoratus*) Very popular hardy annual with a climbing or bushy habit. Very free-flowering in summer, tremendous colour range, blooms often highly scented. 0.3–1.8m/1–6ft. Grow the climbers up tall twiggy sticks or canes. Needs plenty of sun and fertile moist soil. Flower stems must be cut off as flowers die, to encourage further flowering.

• **Zinnia** (*Zinnia elegans*) Half-hardy annual with double flowers in summer in many brilliant colours. 30–90cm/1–3ft. Likes rich soil, sun and shelter from winds.

■ Ten annuals for rock gardens and paving

R ock gardens sometimes look lifeless after the early-flowering alpines have passed their best, but you can add summer colour by a judicious choice of annuals. The following choices are also useful for sowing or planting in gaps between paving stones, to create colourful patches in areas that might otherwise be drab.

• **Candytuft** (*Iberis umbellata*) Popular and very easy hardy annual with heads of pink, red or white flowers. 15–30cm/ 6–12in. Make successional sowing for flowers from early summer to early autumn. Often self-seeds.

• **Livingstone daisy** (*Mesembryanthemum criniflorum*) Half-hardy annual 8cm/3in high, with daisy flowers in many brilliant colours above fleshy leaves. Ideal for a hot, dry spot – needs sun to open its flowers.

• **Pinks (annual)** (*Dianthus chinensis*) Half-hardy annual counterpart of border pinks, with masses of pink, red or white flowers. 15–20cm/6–8in. Likes good soil and plenty of sun.

• **Poached-egg flower** (*Limnanthes douglasii*) Hardy annual with yellow and white flowers. A quick grower, to 38cm/15in. Cool soil but head in sun. Self-sows freely.

• **Sweet alyssum** (*Alyssum maritimum*) Very popular and easy hardy annual with sheets of white or mauve flowers all summer and into autumn. 8–15cm/3–6in. Trim off dead heads: many more blooms will follow.

• **Toadflax** (*Linaria maroccana*) Hardy and easy bushy annual with tiny snapdragon-like flowers in many colours. 20cm/8in. Lots of sun, well-drained soil.

• **Treasure flower** (*Gazania* x *hybrida*) Half-hardy annual with large daisy flowers in many brilliant colours. 20–30cm/8–12in. Needs plenty of sun for a good display. Ideal for hot, dry spot.

• **Viola** (*Viola* hybrids) Half-hardy annual with tiny yellow, blue or purple pansy-like flowers. 15cm/6in. Likes moist soil, will grow well in semi-shade.

• **Violet cress** (*Ionopsidium acaule*) A little-known but excellent hardy annual for filling gaps. Produces tiny pale mauve flowers. 5cm/2in. Needs moist soil and semi-shade: can be scorched in hot sun.

• **Virginian stock** (*Malcolmia maritima*) Highly popular hardy annual, quick and very easy to grow. Scented flowers in red, lilac and white. 20cm/8in. Self-sows.

■ Eight annuals for containers ✓

In tubs, urns, window boxes or hanging baskets, the following plants will make a colourful show all summer and into autumn. Grow in a good potting compost either loam-based or a peat-based type.

• **Floss flower** (*Ageratum houstonianum*) Very popular half-hardy annual, useful for edging. Blue, pink or white powder-puff flowers freely produced, especially if you trim off dead blooms. 15cm/6in. Moist soil, sun.

• **Geranium, ivy-leaf** (*Pelargonium peltatum*) A classic container plant. Half-hardy perennial treated as an annual. Ivy-shaped leaves on trailing stems, producing a cascade of pink, red or white flowers well into autumn. 60cm/2ft. Easy to grow; feed well, plenty of sun.

✓ • **Lobelia** (*Lobelia erinus*) A top-ten half-hardy annual, with masses of blue, carmine or white flowers well into autumn. Choose trailing varieties for containers. 10–20cm/4–8in. Likes moist soil and thrives in partial shade.

✓ • **Nasturtium** (*Tropaeolum majus*) Extremely easy and popular hardy annual. Sow seeds direct in container. Choose trailing varieties, with brilliant flowers in shades of red, orange and yellow. 20cm/8in. Grows in the poorest soils, which improve flowering. Needs lots of sun.

• **Nemesia** (*Nemesia strumosa*) Half-hardy annual with funnel-like flowers in many bright and pastel colours. 20cm/8in. Water plentifully.

✓ • **Petunia** (*Petunia x hybrida*) A top-ten, half-hardy annual with colourful small, medium or large rounded flowers, some bi-coloured or striped. 20–40cm/8–16in. Provide shelter and full sun; a wet summer mars the display.

• **Sweet alyssum** (*Alyssum maritimum*) See p69.

• **Vervain** (*Verbena x hybrida*) See p67.

■ Ten annuals for summer bedding

Bedding plants demand bold and generous treatment. Grow several different kinds together in distinct blocks of contrasting or harmonizing colours.

• **Dahlia, dwarf bedding** (*Dahlia* hybrids) Grown as half-hardy annual from seeds. Wide range of brilliant colours – never out of flower, only stopped by autumn frost. 30–45cm/12–18in. Remove dead flowers. Feed and water well.

• **Geranium, zonal** (*Pelargonium x hortorum*) Grown as half-hardy annual from seeds sown early in year. Flowers produced continuously until autumn frost, in many shades of red, pink, orange, etc. 30–45cm/12–18in. Remove dead flower heads. Plenty of sun needed; feed well.

• **Heliotrope** (*Heliotropium x hybridum*) Popular bedder grown as half-hardy annual. Violet-blue is the most sought-after flower colour. Scented blooms. 30–45cm/12–18in. Needs plenty of sun.

✓ • **Marigold, African and French** (*Tagetes erecta* and *T. patula*) Very popular and easy half-hardy annuals with pungent leaves. African 30–90cm/1–3ft, French 20–30cm/8–12in, both with a continuous display of flowers in shades of yellow, orange or red. Remove dead flowers. Both are sun-lovers.

✓ • **Pansy** (*Viola x wittrockiana*) Grown as half-hardy annual. Rounded flowers in many colours, often with black "faces". Never out of flower. Ideal for partial shade. Height 8–10cm/3–4in.

• **Phlox** (*Phlox drummondii*) Popular half-hardy annual, 15–30cm/6–12in, starry flowers in dense heads, mixture of bright colours. Remove dead flowers, feed well.

• **Scarlet salvia** (*Salvia splendens*) A top-ten half-hardy annual with spikes of brilliant scarlet flowers – almost overpowering when mass-planted. 20–30cm/8–12in. Needs full sun and moist soil.

• **Snapdragon** (*Antirrhinum majus*) Extremely easy and free-flowering half-hardy annual, 25–120cm/10–48in, the dwarfs being best for bedding. Tubular flowers in bold spikes, in mixes of brilliant colours. Best in fertile soil and sun. Pinch out tips of your plants to create bushy habit.

• **Tagetes** (*Tagetes tenuifolia*) Half-hardy annual, 15–20cm/6–8in, rather like a bushy French marigold but without pungent foliage. Masses of tiny single flowers in orange or yellow shades. Needs plenty of sun.

• **Wax begonia** (*Begonia semperflorens*) Highly popular half-hardy annual. Never out of flower. Masses of red, pink or white blooms set against green or bronze foliage. 15–20cm/6–8in. Best in moist soil; tolerates partial shade.

■ Five biennials for spring bedding

Spring-flowering biennials bring early colour to a bedding scheme. All these five are easy to grow, and associate well with spring bulbs such as tulips and hyacinths. They can also be grown in tubs and other containers.

• **Double daisy** (*Bellis perennis* 'Monstrosa') Double pompon flowers in red, pink or white. 15cm/6in. Grow in sun or semi-shade. Often known as Batchelor's Buttons.

• **Forget-me-not** (*Myosotis sylvatica*) Produces a "haze" of tiny blue flowers. 15–20cm/6–8in. Ideal for shade and moist soil. Makes an attractive underplanting for tulips. Seeds itself freely.

• **Polyanthus** (*Primula polyantha*) Produces lots of rounded red, blue, yellow, pink or white flowers. 15–20cm/6–8in. Thrives in partial shade and moist soil. Twigs 15cm/6in high pushed among plants at 30cm/12in intervals will discourage marauding birds.

• **Wallflower** (*Cheiranthus cheiri*) Bushy plants, 30–60cm/1–2ft high, with a long succession of flowers in many brilliant colours (reds, yellows, oranges). Full sun. Avoid wet soils or plants may die.

• **Winter pansy** (*Viola* × *wittrockiana*) The 'Universal' strain is the one to grow; it flowers throughout winter, even when the ground is snow-covered. Shades of blue, yellow and other colours. 15cm/6in. Ideal for partial shade and moist soil.

■ Six half-hardy annuals for sub-tropical bedding

Certain plants have a luxuriant appearance that creates a sub-tropical effect when they are bedded out for the summer. Ideal for a sunny patio bed.

• **Castor-oil plant** (*Ricinus communis*) Large hand-shaped leaves, bronze in some varieties. Insignificant flowers are followed by attractive, spiny seed heads. Vigorous grower, up to 1.5m/5ft. Grows well in shade.

• **Flame nettle** (*Coleus blumei*) Multi-coloured, nettle-like leaves on busy plants – even more bushy if you pinch out tops when young. 20–60cm/8–24in.

• **Indian shot** (*Canna × generalis*) A tender perennial which can be kept for many years if cut down and dug up in autumn and overwintered in pots or boxes of dryish peat in a frost-free place. Brilliant lily-like flowers (red, orange or yellow), and dramatic green, bronze or purple leaves. Up to 1.2m/4ft. Water and feed well.

• **Joseph's coat** (*Amaranthus tricolor*) A bushy foliage plant with brilliantly coloured leaves. 60–90cm/2–3ft. Rich soil is best, and plenty of sun.

• **Ornamental maize** (*Zea mays*) Sweet corn, with colourful broad grassy leaves and/or cobs. Moist soil and plenty of sun.

• **Prince of Wales' feathers** (*Celosia plumosa*) Feathery plumes of red, yellow or apricot flowers. 30–35cm/12–14in. Keep well-watered and fed.

■ Five annuals and biennials for shade and moist soil

Few annuals and biennials grow well in shade. However, these will do well provided that the shade is not too heavy: partial or dappled shade is ideal. They all enjoy soil that stays moist but not wet.

• **Busy Lizzie** (*Impatiens walleriana*) Half-hardy annual now very popular for bedding and containers. It's never out of flower, producing masses of red, pink, white or orange blooms until the first autumn frosts. 30–45cm/12–18in. Remove dead flowers to encourage more to form.

• **Forget-me-not** (*Myosotis sylvatica*) See p71.

• **Monkey flower** (*Mimulus × hybridus*) Half-hardy annual. Becoming very popular, especially for containers. Masses of brilliant red, pink, orange or yellow flowers (often spotted), particularly if you remove dead blooms. 15–20cm/6–8in.

• **Polyanthus** (*Primula polyantha*) See p71.

• **Wax begonia** (*Begonia semperflorens*) See p71.

BORDER PERENNIALS

Border perennials provide long displays of flowers or bold colourful foliage to enhance most parts of the garden. There are two kinds: herbaceous perennials, which die down to the ground each autumn but throw up new shoots with the onset of spring; and evergreen perennials, which retain their leaves (often dramatically textured) all year round, giving interest even in winter. All the plants listed here are herbaceous, unless otherwise stated.

You should cut down the stems of herbaceous perennials each year in late autumn – not to leave "stubble", as is so often seen, but right down to the ground. With evergreens, all you need do is remove any dead leaves. Most perennials thrive in sunny spots with well-drained soil, and are easy-going.

Most should be lifted and split into smaller portions every three or four years to keep them vigorous and free-flowering. Otherwise they need little care apart from annual feeds – use a flower-garden fertilizer. Thin floppy stems vulnerable to being flattened by wind and rain need support from twiggy sticks or proprietary plant supports.

■ **Six perennials which must not be disturbed**

Some perennials do not like root disturbance: once planted they should be left alone, or you may lose them.

• **Campion** (*Lychnis coronaria*) "Shocking" pink flowers contrast beautifully with the grey foliage. Flowers all summer and into autumn. 60cm/2ft. A short-lived perennial for a sunny spot, which usually self-seeds.

• **Chalk plant** (*Gypsophila paniculata*) Produces clouds of tiny white flowers in summer. 90cm/3ft. Good for chalky soils and full sun. Favourite companion for sweet peas.

• **Columbine** (*Aquilegia* hybrids) Favourite cottage-garden plant with spurred flowers, in many colours, from late spring to early summer. 60–90/2–3ft. Short-lived. Enjoys moist soil and sun or partial shade. Self-sows.

• **Lupin** (*Lupinus polyphyllus*) Another favourite, with fat spikes of flowers in many colours during early summer. Russell hybrids are recommended. 0.9–1.2m/3–4ft high. Short-lived plants for acid-neutral soils and sun or partial shade.

• **Peony** (*Paeonia lactiflora*) Early summer display of large globular flowers (pink, red or white). 90cm/3ft. Moist soil, sun or partial shade.

• **Red hot poker** (*Kniphofia* species/varieties) Attractive evergreen with grassy leaves and bold spikes of red, orange,

73

yellow, pale green or cream flowers in late summer/autumn.
0.45–1.2m/1½–4ft. Ideal for hot dry spot. Tie leaves up in
winter to keep crowns dry.

■ Five perennials which need frequent division

These are fast-growing, even rampant, plants which should
be lifted and split every couple of years to prevent them
getting out of hand or deteriorating in quality.

• **Gardener's garters** (*Phalaris arundinacea* 'Picta') A popular
and conspicuous green-and-white striped grass which grows
anywhere. 1m/3ft. Makes a good foil for highly coloured
flowers. Gets out of hand if not divided regularly.

• **Golden rod** (*Solidago* varieties) Sprays of yellow flowers produced in late summer and autumn. 0.45–1.5m/1½–5ft. Older
varieties are more vigorous and spreading than modern ones.
Sun or partial shade, any soil.

• **Lamb's ears** (*Stachys lanata* 'Silver Carpet') Makes marvellous groundcover with its evergreen, silver woolly leaves,
15cm/6in high. Ideal for a hot dry spot.

• **Michaelmas daisy** (*Aster novae-angliae* and *A. novi-belgii*)
Almost a symbol of autumn – masses of daisy-like flowers,
mainly in blues, purples, reds. 0.3–1.5m/1–5ft. Needs a sunny
spot. Support tall ones on twiggy sticks.

• **Yellow loosestrife** (*Lysimachia punctata*) Spikes of yellow
cup-shaped flowers over a long period in summer. 90cm/3ft.
Ideal for poor dry soil – which keeps it in check.

■ Eleven perennials for cutting

If you have the space, it is worth setting aside a special bed
for cutting flowers for flower arrangements. All the ones listed here last well in water.

• **Blanket flower** (*Gaillardia aristata*) Large yellow or orange
daisy flowers in late summer/autumn. 60–90cm/2–3ft. May
need support. Full sun. Avoid wet soil.

• **Carnation** (*Dianthus caryophyllus*) Evergreen. Greyish foliage,
fragrant summer flowers in many colours. 30–60cm/1–2ft.
Good for chalky soils. Not long-lived, so propagate frequently
from summer cuttings.

• **Chalk plant** (*Gypsophila paniculata*) See p73.

• **Coneflower** (*Rudbeckia fulgida*) Large yellow daisy flowers
over a long period in late summer and autumn.
60–90cm/2–3ft. Likes sandy soil and sun. Twiggy sticks
should be given to provide support.

• **Phlox** (*Phlox paniculata*) Popular border plant with clusters
of scented flowers in brilliant or pastel colours,

summer/autumn. 0.6–1.2m/2–4ft. Rich moist soil and partial shade. Ideal for herbaceous borders.

• **Pyrethrum** (*Chrysanthemum coccineum*) Large daisy flowers in carmine, pink or white, early summer. 60–90cm/2–3ft. Ideal for light sandy soil. Needs sun, and sticks for support.

• **Scabious** (*Scabiosa caucasica*) Blue or white "pincushion" flowers in summer. 45–75cm/1½–2½ft. Needs sun. Good for chalky soils.

• **Shasta daisy** (*Chrysanthemum maximum*) Large white daisy flowers in summer/autumn. 90cm/3ft. Grows anywhere. Needs support if not to become sprawling.

• **Sneezeweed** (*Helenium autumnale*) Daisy flowers in yellow or orange shades, late summer and autumn. 60–90cm/2–3ft. Sun and good drainage needed.

• **Tickseed** (*Coreopsis verticillata* 'Grandiflora') Profusion of yellow daisy flowers in summer and autumn, feathery foliage. 60–75cm/2–2½ft. Best on sandy soil, full sun.

• **Yarrow** (*Achillea filipendulina* 'Coronation Gold') Flat heads of yellow flowers in summer and autumn, very long flowering period. 90cm/3ft. Ideal for hot dry spot.

■ Five perennials for shade and dry soil

These conditions are typically found under large trees whose roots dry out the soil and whose canopy of branches create shade. The combination of shade and dryness is difficult to most plants, but the following will thrive.

• **Barrenwort** (*Epimedium* species) Groundcover plant with dainty sprays of tiny yellow, rose-pink, orange or white spring flowers. Attractive foliage – often tinted with red or bronze in spring. 20–30cm/8–12in.

• **Dead nettle** (*Lamium maculatum*) Evergreen groundcover plant with attractive silver-striped foliage. Spikes of pink or white flowers, depending on the variety, appear in spring or early summer. 15–30cm/6–12in.

• **London pride** (*Saxifraga umbrosa*) Favourite old cottage-garden plant with evergreen foliage growing in rosette form (good groundcover) and sprays of pale pink flowers in spring. 45cm/18in when in flower.

• **Lungwort** (*Pulmonaria* species) Groundcover perennials with blue, pink or white flowers in spring. Leaves are heavily spotted with silver in some varieties. 30cm/12in.

• **Yellow archangel** (*Galeobdolon luteum* 'Variegatum') Rampant evergreen groundcover plant with silver-splashed foliage and yellow flowers in spring. 30cm/12in. Easily controlled by pulling it from the ground.

■ Six perennials for shade and moist soil

There are many lovely plants for soil which does not dry out and receives dappled shade – in other words, shade cast by trees with a light canopy of foliage. Typical areas are light woodland or parts of a shrub border. Work plenty of peat or well-rotted organic matter into the soil for these plants.

• **Candelabra primulas** (*Primula* species) Whorls of flowers up the stems in early summer. Various colours, such as red *Primula japonica*. 60–90cm/2–3ft.

• **Drumstick primrose** (*Primula denticulata*) This has large globular heads of mauve, pink or white flowers over a long period in spring. 30cm/12in. Easy and reliable.

• **Ferns** There are many hardy ferns with deciduous or ever-green foliage (fronds) which create a cool effect. In spring the bright green fronds uncurl attractively. The following popular and easy ferns also have a lovely golden-brown colour in autumn: Lady Fern (*Athyrium filix-femina*), deciduous, around 60cm/2ft; Male Fern (*Dryopteris felix-mas*), deciduous, around 60cm/2ft; Soft Shield Fern (*Polystichum setiferum*), evergreen, 60–90cm/2–3ft.

• **Lily-of-the-valley** (*Convallaria majalis*) Favourite old cottage-garden plant with white, scented bell-like flowers in spring. 15cm/6in. Vigorous in moist conditions.

• **Plantain lily** (*Hosta* species and varieties) Grown for their large dramatic leaves which may be green, bluish, gold or var-iegated. Lily-like lilac or white flowers are produced in sum-mer. Heights variable.

• **Solomon's seal** (*Polygonatum multiflorum*) White and green bell-like flowers on arching stems in late spring. Attractive foliage. 90cm/3ft.

■ Five perennials for hot dry places

These plants are for positions in full sun, where the soil dries out in summer, that will prosper even in arid condi-tions. To create a more dramatic effect, cover the soil with stone chippings or shingle.

• **Anthemis** (*Anthemis cupaniana*) Attractive 30cm/12in high perennial with evergreen greyish ferny foliage and white daisy flowers all summer and into autumn.

• **Cinquefoils** (*Potentilla* varieties) Red or yellow flowers, like small single roses, in summer. Very long flowering period. 45cm/18in.

• **Jerusalem sage** (*Phlomis fruticosa*) A shrubby, spreading plant with grey-green woolly evergreen foliage and whorls of yellow hooded flowers in summer. 90cm/3ft.

• **Stonecrop** (*Sedum spectabile*) Succulent plant with fleshy greyish leaves and flat heads of long-lasting pink flowers in autumn. 30–45cm/12–18in.

• **Valerian** (*Centranthus ruber*) Pink or white flowers in clustered heads produced over a long period in summer. Greyish green foliage. 60cm/2ft.

■ Eight perennials for the mixed border

The following perennials are subdued in colour, and will look good when planted around shrubs, either to harmonize or to present a quiet contrast.

• **Bearded iris** (*Iris germanica* hybrids) Spikes of flowers, vast colour range, early summer. Evergreen sword-shaped leaves. Up to 90cm/3ft. Full sun, light soil.

• **Bear's breeches** (*Acanthus mollis*) Dramatic, deeply cut foliage and spikes of white and purple hooded flowers in summer. 90cm/3ft. Needs fertile soil and sun.

• **Cranesbill** (*Geranium* species and varieties) Pink, white, purple or blue rounded flowers over a long period in summer. 30–60cm/1–2ft. Good groundcover.

• **Day lily** (*Hemerocallis* hybrids) Lily-like flowers, each lasting only one day, but in long succession in summer and autumn. Vast range of colours. 60–90cm/2–3ft. Fertile soil, sun or partial shade. Protect young growth from slugs.

• **Delphinium** (*Delphinium elatum* hybrids) Bold spikes of blue, purple, pink or white flowers in summer. To 1.8m/6ft. Support each spike with a bamboo cane. Rich deep soil, sun and shelter from winds.

• **Globe thistle** (*Echinops ritro*) Large globular steel-blue flowers in summer. Attractively cut leaves 0.9–1.2m/3–4ft. Needs support. Full sun.

• **Pampas grass** (*Cortaderia selloana*) Large evergreen grass, forming huge clumps, with plumes of silvery long-lasting flowers in autumn. Up to 2.4m/8ft. Full sun.

• **Sea holly** (*Eryngium planum*) Globular blue flowers in summer. 60cm/2ft. Needs a little support. For sun and poor soil.

Ten perennials with a long flowering period

Many perennials are long-flowering, but the examples given here are exceptionally so. They are especially recommended for small gardens where the limited space needs to be used to best advantage.

• **Avens** (*Geum chiloense*) Red or yellow flowers, like small single roses, in summer. 45–60cm/1½–2ft. Sun or part shade, and peaty soil.

• **Bellflower** (*Campanula* species/varieties) Bell-shaped flowers in blue or white, summer. Heights variable – average 90cm/3ft. Needs support. Fertile soil, and sun or partial shade.

• **Flax** (*Linum perenne*) Blue flowers in summer. Up to 45cm/18in. Full sun, any well-drained soil. Somewhat lax growth needs a little support.

• **Knotweed** (*Polygonum bistorta* 'Superbum') Produces spikes of pink flowers over a long period in summer 90cm/3ft. Adaptable but likes sun.

• **Lady's mantle** (*Alchemilla mollis*) Clouds of lime-green flowers all summer. 30cm/12in. For sun or partial shade, and moist soil. Self-sows freely unless clipped over before seeds formed.

• **Oenothera** (*Oenothera fruticosa*) Produces a succession of yellow cup-shaped flowers throughout summer. 30–60cm/1–2ft. Needs sun, and twiggy sticks for support.

• **Penstemon** (*Penstemon* x *gloxinioides*) Spikes of tubular flowers in ruby-red and many other colours during summer and autumn. 60–90cm/2–3ft. Not too hardy – needs sun, and cloche protection during winter.

• **Salvia** (*Salvia superba* 'East Friesland') Produces spikes of violet-blue flowers during summer and autumn. 60–75cm/2–2½ft. Likes sun and sandy soil.

• **Speedwell** (*Veronica spicata*) Spikes of many small sky-blue flowers in summer. 45cm/18in. Moist soil and sun/part shade. Twiggy sticks for support.

• **Spiderwort** (*Tradescantia* x *andersoniana*) Blue, purple, rose and white three-petalled flowers in summer and autumn. Grassy foliage. 60cm/2ft. Moist soil, and sun or partial shade.

■ **Seven perennials for winter or spring flowers**

These plants are suitable for growing around the base of winter- or spring-flowering shrubs, for bright splashes of colour in the border.

• **Bleeding heart** (*Dicentra spectabilis*) Pink and white heart-shaped flowers in spring above attractive foliage. 45–60cm/1½–2ft. A pure white form is becoming popular. Moist peaty soil and dappled shade.

• **Christmas rose** (*Helleborus niger*) Evergreen hand-shaped leaves and white single-rose-like flowers in winter. 30cm/12in. Fertile moist soil and partial shade.

• **Elephant's ears** (*Bergenia* species/varieties) Large, shiny, leathery evergreen foliage and dense heads of pink, red or white flowers in spring. 30cm/12in. Foliage often turns reddish in winter. Moist soil. Sun or partial shade.

• **Lenten rose** (*Helleborus orientalis*) Evergreen hand-shaped leaves and cup-shaped purple, pink, cream or white flowers, often spotted, in late winter/early spring. 45–60cm/1½–2ft. Fertile moist soil, partial shade.

• **Leopard's bane** (*Doronicum caucasicum*) Yellow daisy flowers in spring. 45cm/1½ft. Moist fertile soil, sun or partial shade.

• **Spurge** (*Euphorbia epithymoides*) Acid-yellow flowers in spring. 45cm/1½ft. Best in light soil and full sun.

• **Winter iris** (*Iris unguicularis*) Deep-green, grassy, evergreen leaves and soft blue flowers in winter. 30cm/12in. Good on poor soils, including chalk. Needs full sun. Slow to establish.

■ **Six perennials for autumn colour**

Many gardens are sadly lacking in perennials that show their best in autumn. Some of the following should be in every garden.

• **African lily** (*Agapanthus campanulatus*) Heads of tubular pale blue or white flowers, strap-shaped leaves. 60–75cm/2–2½ft. Sheltered site in full sun; fertile soil.

• **Chinese lantern** (*Physalis alkekengi franchetii*) Orange lantern-like fruits can be dried for winter decoration. 60cm/2ft. Grows anywhere. Rather rampant.

• **Gladwyn iris** (*Iris foetidissima*) Evergreen, grassy leaves, purple flowers in summer, and brilliant orange seeds in autumn. 45cm/18in high. Moist peaty soil and shade.

• **Japanese anemone** (*Anemone* x *hybrida*) Pink, single-rose-like flowers, or white in some varieties. 60–90cm/2–3ft. Ideal for chalky soil and partial shade.

• **Michaelmas daisy** (*Aster*) See p74.

• **Peruvian lily** (*Alstroemeria aurantiaca*) Brilliant orange-scarlet, pink or yellow lily-like flowers, tuberous roots. 90cm/3ft. Ideal for sandy soil and full sun. Young plants establish better than dormant tubers.

■ **Six perennials with beautiful leaves**

Attractive leaves make a good contrast for flowering perennials and shrubs.

• **Dwarf bamboo** (*Arundinaria viridistriata*) Knee-high non-invasive bamboo with acid-yellow leaves striped green. 1.5m/5ft. Ordinary soil, sun or dappled shade. Cut down stems in late winter.

• **Moor grass** (*Molinia caerulea* 'Variegata') Dwarf grass with cream and green striped leaves. 60cm/2ft. Full sun for best colour. Well-drained soil.

• **New Zealand flax** (*Phormium* species/varieties) Bold ever-green, sword-like leaves, highly coloured in many varieties – some striped red or yellow. Heights 0.3–1.8m/1–6ft. Need very good drainage, and sun for best colour.

• **Plantain lily** (*Hosta*) See p76.

• **White sage** (*Artemisia ludoviciana*) Silvery-grey feathery foliage. 1.2m/4ft. An ideal plant for hot, dry, even arid spots.

• **Zebra grass** (*Miscanthus sinensis* 'Zebrinus') Ornamental grass with beautiful gold-banded arching leaves. 1.8m/6ft. Any soil, full sun. Cut down the stems in early spring.

■ Five perennials for containers

The following will grow well in tubs on the patio. Grow them in a good loam-based potting compost, such as John Innes No. 2. Keep well-watered in summer.

• **African lily** (*Agapanthus campanulatus*) See p79. Good autumn colour.

• **Day lily** (*Hemerocallis* hybrids) See p77. Long-flowering.

• **New Zealand flax** (*Phormium* species/varieties) See above. Dramatic colourful leaves.

• **Plantain lily** (*Hosta* species/varieties) See p76. For positions in shade and moist soil.

• **Spurge** (*Euphorbia wulfenii*) A large plant for a large tub. Up to 1.2m/4ft. Attractive grey-green leaves and, in spring and summer, large heads of tiny flowers surrounded by prominent greenish-yellow bracts. For sun or semi-shade.

BULBS AND CORMS

Bulbs and corms are virtually guaranteed to flower, with a minimum of soil preparation, as the flower buds are already formed inside them when they are planted. If you give them the right conditions, they will bloom regularly each year.

Because, on the whole, bulbs and corms are rela-tively inexpensive compared with, say, shrubs, you can afford to mass-plant them, which certainly creates the best effect. Spring bulbs are so well known that many gardeners do not realize that there are bulbs and corms that can be planted for flowering at other sea-sons – not just in spring, which is the peak time. Spring-flowering bulbs are planted in autumn, sum-mer-flowering bulbs in spring, and autumn-flowering bulbs in summer.

Corms have a different botanical structure from bulbs, but they often look similar and are planted and

grown in the same way. A third category is tubers – plants with "tuberous" or fleshy roots, such as dahlias.

Bulbs, corms and tubers are all types of food and water storage organs which supply the plants during their resting periods.

Almost all bulbs, corms and tubers are easy to grow. The main thing to guard against is removing the leaves before they have died down naturally, as this will result in fewer flowers the following year.

■ Four bulbs and corms for shade

Most bulbous plants are sun-lovers, but there are a few that will thrive in permanent shade, provided that it isn't too heavy. The dappled shade cast by trees is ideal.

• **Cyclamen** (*Cyclamen hederifolium*) A charming miniature hardy cyclamen, 10cm/4in high, with pink flowers appearing before the leaves in late summer/autumn. The leaves make attractive groundcover. Likes well-drained humus-rich soil.

• **English bluebell** (*Endymion nonscriptus*) Spikes of mid-blue bell-like flowers in spring. 30cm/12in. Vigorous habit – can almost become a weed. Prefers acid or lime-free soil.

• **Snowdrop** (*Galanthus nivalis*) White bell-like flowers in winter. 15cm/6in. Likes heavy, moist, rich soil. Best planted immediately after flowering.

• **Spanish bluebell** (*Endymion hispanicus*) Spikes of bell-like flowers in blue (also pink and white) in spring. 45cm/18in. Vigorous habit. Flowers are bluebell-scented. Best in an acid soil but will grow in chalky earth.

■ Sixteen bulbs and corms for the mixed or shrub border

Some bulbous plants look especially effective when used in a border to harmonize or contrast with shrubs or hardy perennials. The best plan is to plant them in bold drifts. Many will naturalize and spread themselves over the years.

• *Anemone blanda* Blue, red, pink or white daisy flowers, forming a carpet if mass-planted, produced in spring. 15cm/6in. Likes peaty soil, and sun or partial shade.

• *Anemone coronaria* Large poppy-like flowers (sometimes called poppy anemone), in red, blue, pink, during spring or summer. 15–30cm/6–12in high. Blooms are excellent for cutting. Ideal for warm sunny well-drained border.

• **Autumn crocus** (*Colchicum speciosum*) Not a true crocus, but has crocus-like, lilac-coloured flowers in the autumn. 30cm/12in high when in leaf – the large leaves appear in spring and take up a lot of space. Sun or partial shade.

• **Crown imperial** (*Fritillaria imperialis*) Clusters of large orange bells appear in spring on 90cm/3ft high stems. Fertile well-drained soil, sun or partial shade. Plant the bulbs on their side if the soil is heavy.

• **Dahlia** (*Dahlia variabilis*) Border dahlias grow from fleshy tubers and flower in late summer. They look better with hardy perennials than with shrubs. Tender: must be dug up before winter, and dormant tubers must be overwintered in frost-free conditions. Vast range of varieties, flowers in all shapes, sizes and colours. Heights 0.6–1.5m/2–5ft. Ideal for cutting. Feed and water well in summer.

• **Daffodil** (*Narcissus* hybrids) Another large and diverse group, although the golden trumpet varieties are probably most popular. Spring-flowering. 30–60cm/1–2ft. Foliage can be cut off 6 weeks after flowers have faded with no ill effect. Don't tie them up or knot them. Moist fertile soil, and sun or dappled shade.

• **Dutch iris** (*Iris xiphium* hybrids) Yellow, white, blue or purple flowers produced on strong stems during summer. 30–45cm/12–18in. Flowers good for cutting. Well-drained soil and full sun. Good for rock gardens.

• **Kaffir lily** (*Schizostylis coccinea*) Red or pink star-shaped flowers in spikes in autumn, good for cutting. 60–90cm/2–3ft. Needs a warm sunny spot with very well-drained yet moist soil – a border under a warm wall is ideal.

• **Lilies** (*Lilium* species/hybrids) Hundreds of species and varieties. Among the most popular are the mid-century hybrids, such as orange 'Enchantment', with upturned flowers. 0.6–1.8m/2–6ft. There are varieties for both acid and chalky soils. All like good drainage. Add plenty of peat or well-rotted organic matter before planting. The roots should be shaded, the heads in the sun.

• **Nerine** (*Nerine bowdenii*) Bright pink, trumpet-shaped flowers in late summer and early autumn. 60cm/2ft high, the leaves appearing after the flowers. Needs a warm, sunny, very well-drained border, as it's only moderately hardy. Provide rich soil and don't disturb after planting.

• **Ornamental onion** (*Allium cernuum*) Loose heads of small pink flowers in spring and summer. 60cm/2ft. Ideal for warm well-drained border with plenty of sun.

• **Spring snowflake** (*Leucojum vernum*) White and green bell-like flowers in spring. 20cm/8in. Moist soil. Sun or partial shade. Like a later-flowering, and larger, snowdrop.

• **Squill** (*Scilla sibirica*) Dainty blue bell-like flowers in late winter/spring. 10–15cm/4–6in. Easy-going in well-drained soil and sun or partial shade.

• **Summer hyacinth** (*Galtonia candicans*) Bold spikes of white bell-like flowers in summer. 1.2m/4ft. Fertile soil. Sun or partial shade. Watch out for slugs.

• **Summer snowflake** (*Leucojum aestivum*) White bell-like flowers which, despite the common name, appear in spring. 60cm/2ft. Moist soil. Sun or partial shade.

• **Tiger flower** (*Tigridia pavonia*) Large, three-petalled summer flowers in many bright colours, often heavily spotted. 45–60cm/1½–2ft. Needs warm sunny sheltered border with rich soil. Not too hardy: in cold areas, lift in autumn and keep indoors over winter.

■ Three bulbs and corms for growing in grass

G rassy areas can be made colourful by planting bulbs and corms, perhaps around the bases of trees or on banks. Do not cut the grass until at least 6 weeks after the flowers have faded, or there will be few or no flowers next year.

• **Crocus, large-flowered Dutch** Large, goblet-shaped flower in shades of yellow, purples, blue or white in spring. 10–15cm/4–6in. Full sun needed for blooms to open.

• **Crocus, autumn-flowering** (*Crocus speciosus*) Lilac flowers in autumn, leaves following in spring. 10cm/4in. Full sun and well-drained soil.

• **Daffodil, miniature** (*Narcissus bulbocodium* and *N. cyclamineus*) Yellow flared and trumpet-shaped miniature flowers respectively, in spring. 15cm/6in. Moist soil, and sun or partial shade. Plant generously in drifts.

■ Nine bulbs and corms for the rock garden

M any of the miniatures are ideal for providing colour among the alpines at various times of year. Plant them in little groups of five to ten.

• **Crocus** (*Crocus chrysanthus* varieties) These are miniature crocuses, 8cm/3in high, with flowers in various colours (including yellows and blues) in late winter/early spring. Plenty of sun needed.

• **Glory of the snow** (*Chionodoxa luciliae*) Masses of starry blue flowers in early spring. 8–15cm/3–6in. Full sun needed.

• **Grape hyacinth** (*Muscari armeniacum*) Thick short spikes of long-lasting blue flowers in spring. Rather lax, grassy leaves. 20cm/8in. Plenty of sun needed.

• **Iris** (*Iris danfordiae* and *I. reticulata*) Miniature irises with yellow and blue flowers respectively during late winter. 10–15cm/4–6in. *I. danfordiae* does not always flower in 2nd year. Plenty of sun, light sandy soil.

• **Ornamental onion** (*Allium moly*) Clusters of small, yellow, starry flowers. 30cm/12in. Warm sunny well-drained border – ideal for hot dry spot. Often spreads by self-sowing.

• **Quamash** (*Camassia quamash*) Spikes of violet-blue flowers in late spring/early summer. 45cm/18in. Likes moist heavy soil and partial shade.

• **Puschkinia** (*Puschkinia libanotica*) Pale and deep blue starry flowers in spring. 10–15cm/4–6in. Needs peaty soil, and position in sun or partial shade.

• **Sternbergia** (*Sternbergia lutea*) Deep yellow crocus-like flowers in autumn; leaves later. 10–15cm/4–6in. Needs a warm sunny spot with good drainage.

• **Winter aconite** (*Eranthis hyemalis*) Yellow cup-shaped flowers in late winter. Ferny foliage. 10cm/4in. Moist soil needed and partial shade.

■ Three bulbs and corms for containers

The following are recommended for growing in tubs and window boxes where they will provide plenty of colour for seasonal displays. Use a good loam-based compost such as John Innes No. 2 or soilless.

• **Begonia, tuberous** (*Begonia* x *tuberhybrida*) Huge double flowers in many brilliant or pastel colours throughout summer. Height about 30cm/12in. Tender, so overwinter dormant tubers in a frost-free place. Needs sun and plenty of water.

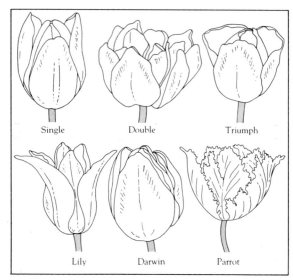

Single   Double   Triumph

Lily   Darwin   Parrot

• **Hyacinth** (*Hyacinthus orientalis* hybrids) Produce thick spikes of highly fragrant, bell-shaped blue, pink, red or white flowers in spring. 25–30cm/10–12in. Provide a position with plenty of sun and a container and compost with good drainage.

• **Tulip, dwarf** (*Tulipa greigii* and *T. kaufmanniana* hybrids) Cup-shaped flowers in brilliant colours (especially reds and yellows) during spring. 20cm/8in. These hybrids are ideal for containers. Leaves of some varieties mottled with bronze. Sun or part shade, good drainage.

■ Three bulbous plants for the formal garden

Some bulbs and corms have been so vigorously cross-bred over the years that they are far removed from the original wild species. These manmade plants are very formal-looking, and are thus not always easy to use in the garden. However, the two described here, along with a third, wild species, are great favourites for their exquisite colours and flower forms.

• **Gladiolus** (*Gladiolus* hybrids) Tall bold spikes of flowers in summer and early autumn, used mainly for cutting. Grow in their own bed, or perhaps in a row in a vegetable garden. Various groups, including large-flowered and smaller-flowered primulinus and butterfly hybrids. All come in a vast colour range. 90–120cm/3–4ft. Grow in warm sunny spot in well-cultivated fertile soil. Feed and water well in summer. Support each spike with a bamboo cane. Lift the corms in autumn, dry off and store in a frost-proof place for the winter. Planting time is early spring.

• **Tulip, large-flowered hybrids** (*Tulipa* hybrids) Used mainly for spring bedding in formal arrangements, often with under-planting of wallflowers (*Cheiranthus cheiri*) or forget-me-nots (*Myosotis sylvatica*). The many types include: SINGLE EARLY TULIPS, 15–30cm/6–12in, with single cup-shaped flowers; DOUBLE EARLY TULIPS, same height but fully double blooms; TRIUMPH TULIPS, 45cm/18in, large angular blooms on strong stems; DARWIN HYBRIDS, 60cm/2ft, large goblet-shaped blooms; LILY-FLOWERED TULIPS, 45–60cm/1½–2ft, long pointed petals, blooms resembling those of a waterlily (*Nymphaea*); PARROT TULIPS, 45–60cm/1½–2ft, twisted and frilled petals, often bi-coloured; DOUBLE LATE TULIPS, 45–60cm/1½–2ft, double blooms. All these come in many colours – reds, pinks, yellows, oranges, cream, white, even near-black, and from subdued pastels to strong vibrant shades. Best grown in full sun but will flower in partial shade. Sheltered spot desirable for tall varieties. Any ordinary soil will do, but must be well-drained. Chalky or limy soils particularly good.

• **Giant onion** (*Allium giganteum*) Round, lilac-purple flower heads on 1.2m/4ft stems, summer. Stately. Plant group of 5 or 7, well-drained soil, sunny spot.

EXOTICS

Exotics – from warm or tropical regions of the world – have luxurious associations for inhabitants of cooler climes. Most have to be nurtured under glass in temperate climates. A warm greenhouse or conservatory (minimum temperature 15°C/59°F), or an intermediate one (at least 8°C/50°F), allows you to grow some highly colourful tropical plants. Even a cool greenhouse or conservatory (at least 5–7°C/40–45°F) can be colourful all year round.

■ Five flowering exotics for the warm greenhouse

These plants offer long-lasting, spectacular flowers. They are easy to grow provided that they have plenty of warmth at all times, and moist or humid air.

• **African violet** (*Saintpaulia ionantha*) Single or double violet-like flowers in shades of blue, purple, violet, pink, red and white, above a rosette of downy, deep green leaves. Flowers virtually all year. 10cm/4in. Likes soilless compost and humid air. Avoid wet compost.

• **Glory bush** (*Tibouchina semidecandra*) Evergreen shrub, 3m/10ft tall, with blue-purple flowers in summer/autumn. Stems should be cut back hard in late winter. Can be kept smaller by regular pruning.

• **Madagascar jasmine** (*Stephanotis floribunda*) Tall climber with waxy, white, highly scented flowers from spring to autumn. Enjoys slight humidity. Ideal for back wall of conservatory. 5m/15ft. Prune back in late winter to reduce height.

• **Oleander** (*Nerium oleander*) Evergreen shrub, 1.8m/6ft high, with red, pink or purplish-red funnel-shaped or fully, double lobed flowers in summer and autumn. Likes plenty of sun and fresh air.

• **Zebra plant** (*Aphelandra squarrosa* 'Louisae') Small evergreen shrub with large, white-striped leaves and bright yellow pyramid-shaped flowers. 1m/3ft. Likes high humidity. Prune back stems after flowering.

■ Five foliage exotics for the warm greenhouse

Prized for their attractive leaves, these plants like plenty of warmth and a humid or moist atmosphere.

• **Begonia** (*Begonia rex*) Large leaves heavily patterned with various colours (pink, red, purple, maroon, silver and cream). 30–45cm/1–1½ft. Best grown in peat-based potting compost. Be sparing with water. Shade from bright sunlight.

• **Cabbage palm** (*Cordyline terminalis*) Long sword-like leaves in bronze-red or rich purple; young leaves may be cream edged with pink. 90cm/3ft. Not fussy as to growing medium – grow in loam-based or soilless potting compost.

• **Croton** (*Codiaeum variegatum pictum*) Evergreen shrub with leaves in various sizes, shapes and colours. Usually has brilliant multi-coloured foliage (shades of red, yellow, copper). 60cm/2ft and more. Grows well in soilless compost.

• **Dragon lily** (*Dracaena deremensis*) Evergreen shrub with sword-shaped leaves, deep green striped with silver. 1.2m/4ft. Grows well in peat-based compost.

• **Philodendron** (*Philodendron species*) Shrubs and climbers with large, often deeply cut, deep green shiny leaves. 2-3m/6–10ft. Grow well in peat-based potting compost. Climbers need support of a moss-pole.

■ Five flowering exotics for the intermediate greenhouse

These highly popular greenhouse plants have a long succession of colourful flowers. All are easy to grow.

• **Abutilon** (*Abutilon* hybrids) Evergreen shrubs with pendulous, bell-shaped flowers in shades of red, yellow, orange or pink. Large maple-like leaves. 1.2–1.8m/4–6ft. Cut hard back in early spring to keep compact. Grow in John Innes potting compost No. 2.

• **Brunfelsia** (*Brunfelsia calycina*) Evergreen shrub of modest proportions, with masses of large fragrant blue-purple flowers in summer. 60cm/2ft. Pinch out tip of young plant for bushy habit. Grow in John Innes potting compost No. 2.

• **Cyclamen** (*Cyclamen persicum* hybrids) Marvellous winter pot plants with flowers in shades of red, pink or white. Some are scented, and in some varieties the foliage is heavily marbled with silver. 10–20cm/4–8in. Dry off plants for the summer to let them rest. Grow cyclamen in a peaty compost.

• **Paper flower** (*Bougainvillea spectabilis*) A popular climber with bright purple, orange, white or reddish papery bracts in summer. 2.4m/8ft. Likes plenty of sun and humidity and humus-rich compost. Prune early spring – cut out weak shoots and reduce other shoots by about one-third.

• **Shrubby mallow** (*Hibiscus rosa-sinensis*) Deciduous shrub with succession of large flowers that appear throughout the summer – red, pink, yellow, orange. Reaches 1.8m/6ft. Grow in John Innes potting compost No. 2.

■ Five foliage exotics for the intermediate greenhouse

All the following have attractive leaves which contrast well with adjacent flowering plants. Again, easy to grow.

• **Asparagus fern** (*Asparagus sprengeri*) An evergreen perennial with cascading, bright green feathery foliage, ideal for front of staging or hanging baskets. 1m/3ft. Likes humid conditions and moisture-retentive peaty compost.

• **Bromeliads** Most popular are the urn plant, which has a vase-like arrangement of broad grey leaves; and the flaming sword, of similar habit but with brown-banded leaves. 0.5–1m/20in–3ft. Keep the "vases" filled with fresh water. Grow in peaty compost and provide humidity in warm conditions. Grow new plants from offsets.

• **Ferns** Lush, green, ferny foliage makes a good foil for brightly coloured flowers. Particularly recommended: *Adiantum raddianum*, a maidenhair fern, pale green fronds and black stalks, 30–45cm/12–18in; *Asplenium bulbiferum*, a spleenwort, fine-cut fronds with little plantlets on them, 45–60cm/1½–2ft; *Nephrolepis exaltata*, sword fern, pale green, deeply cut fronds, arching habit, 45–75cm/1½–2½ft. Use a peat-based potting compost and provide humidity and shade.

• **Flame nettle** (*Coleus blumei*) Bright multi-coloured foliage. Raised from seed sown in spring each year. Pinch out tips of young plants for bushy specimens. 45cm/1½ft. Grow in soilless compost. Dry air, dryness at roots and scorching sunlight are not tolerated and likely to turn plants brown. Most grow well under greenhouse staging.

• **Mother-in-law's tongue** (*Sansevieria trifasciata* 'Laurentii') Evergreen perennial with 90cm/3ft erect sword-shaped leaves edged with yellow. Likes dry air, moderate watering and gritty John Innes compost.

■ Five flowering exotics for the cool greenhouse

This is a popular selection from the huge range of plants suitable for cool conditions (at least 5–7°C/40–45°F).

• **Bird of paradise flower** (*Strelitzia reginae*) Large, broad, evergreen banana-like leaves and striking blue and orange bird's-head-like flowers in summer/autumn. 1.8m/6ft. Will flower only after 4–5 years. Likes plenty of sun and soil-based compost. Avoid damaging tap-root when potting young plants, or flowering will be delayed.

• **Cape primrose** (*Streptocarpus* hybrids) Clump-forming evergreen perennials with tubular flowers in various colours, summer and autumn. 25cm/10in. Humidity, shade and peaty compost. Keep dryish during winter rest.

• **Cineraria** (*Senecio* x *hybridus*) Very popular short-term pot plant for winter/spring flowers. Large heads of daisy-like flowers in shades of blue, purple, pink, red. 15–45cm/6in–1½ft. Provide lots of fresh air and check for aphids and whitefly. Dislikes soggy compost and too much heat.

• **Fuchsia** Bushy, deciduous shrubs which flower prolifically throughout summer and into autumn. Bell-like flowers in blue, pink, red, white. 0.75–2m/1½–3ft. Best to raise new plants each year from summer cuttings. Grow in peat-based compost.

• **Regal pelargonium** (*Pelargonium domesticum*) Compact bushy plants which flower profusely in summer – large flowers in shades of red, pink, mauve, purple. 30–45cm/1–1½ft. Normally raised anew each year from summer cuttings. Best in loam-based compost. Likes dry air.

■ Four foliage exotics for the cool greenhouse

There are many good foliage plants for growing in cool conditions, but the following easy and reliable kinds should have a place in every collection.

• **Ivy** (*Hedera helix* varieties) Can be grown as trailers or climbers. Small evergreen leaves, either plain green or variegated. 1.2–5m/4–15ft. Good for trailing over edge of staging: don't keep it too wet. Peat-based compost suitable. Many varieties available, with differently patterned and coloured leaves.

• **Silk oak** (*Grevillea robusta*) A tree (which remains small when pot-grown) with ferny green foliage. 3–4m/10–13ft. Best in a slightly acid or lime-free compost.

• **Spider plant** (*Chlorophytum comosum* 'Variegatum') Evergreen perennial with grassy green-and-white striped leaves, and cascades of little plantlets on long stems. 30cm/1ft. Vigorous grower, so pot on regularly in peaty compost.

• **Wandering Jew** (*Tradescantia fluminensis* 'Quicksilver') Evergreen trailer with white-and-green striped leaves. 5cm/2in. Grow in peaty compost and replace regularly from cuttings taken in summer (easy to root).

■ Three exotic shrubs for the garden

In warmer temperate climates, the following will thrive in a warm sunny sheltered spot in the garden.

• **Bottle brush** (*Grevillea sulphurea*) A 1.8m/6ft evergreen shrub with yellow bottle-brush-like flowers from spring to early autumn. Needs acid (lime-free) peaty soil; ideally grown against a warm, sunny wall.

• **Cabbage tree** (*Cordyline australis*) An evergreen, palm-like shrub with long, narrow grey-green leaves. Can reach 7.5m/25ft, forming a thick trunk. Likes full sun and fertile well-drained soil.

• **Chilean fire bush** (*Embothrium coccineum*) Large shrub or small tree, evergreen, bearing brilliant scarlet blooms in spring/early summer. 10m/30ft. Variety *lanceolatum* is hardier. Needs acid (lime-free) soil and full sun.

■ Three exotic climbers for the garden

These are spectacular flowering climbers for a warm, sunny sheltered wall. Support the stems by tying them to horizontal wires fixed to the wall.

• **Fremontodendron** (*Fremontodendron californicum*)
Deciduous, producing large, cup-shaped, deep yellow flowers between late spring and mid-autumn. 2.4–3.6m/8–12ft. Prefers light sandy soil.

• **Passion flower** (*Passiflora caerulea*) Vigorous evergreen to at least 6m/20ft. Intricate blue and white flowers between early summer and early autumn. Needs well-drained soil. Thin out oldest stems in late winter.

• **Trumpet vine** (*Campsis radicans*) Vigorous deciduous climber – can attain at least 9m/30ft. Self-clinging stems carry large orange and scarlet trumpet-shaped blooms, late summer/early autumn. Fertile, well-drained soil. Previous year's shoots should be cut back to 3–4 buds in early spring to encourage a good show of flowers.

CLIMBERS AND WALL SHRUBS

As well as being invaluable for giving height to an otherwise flat plot, climbers and wall shrubs also offer an excellent way to disguise an ugly enclosure or hide unsightly objects. To grow well, all need some means of support – a wall or fence, or perhaps a rustic arch or pergola erected purely for the plants' convenience.

The so-called "self-clinging" types have either aerial roots (the ivy) or sucker pads (Virginia creeper). Other climbers (such as grape vines) have tendrils. Ramblers (such as honeysuckle) push toward the light by twining around a host plant. Some shrubs, although not strictly climbers, adopt an upright habit when grown against a wall – for example, *Pyracantha*.

Instead of treating climbers in isolation, consider their relationship with other plants nearby – especially in their flowering habits. One approach is to mix flowering times – for example, grow an early-flowering clematis on a late-flowering tree or shrub, such as a browny-red smoke bush (*Cotinus coggygria*). Alternatively, you can mix colours in a pair that flower simultaneously – say, white *Clematis montana* over a scarlet hawthorn.

Plant at least 30cm/12in from a wall or 45cm/18in from a tree. Guide the young stem to the support with an angled bamboo cane. Prune early-flowering climbers immediately flowering is over. If you wait until autumn, when you prune your other climbers, you will cut off next spring's flowering buds.

■ Eight supports for climbers

Wood supports should be treated with a preservative (not creosote, which gives off toxic fumes) and left for 2 weeks before use.

• **Horizontal wires** (at 30–45cm/1–1½ft intervals) supported on stout "vine eyes" screwed into brickwork or timber.

• **Trellis panels,** either freestanding or wall-mounted (with a gap of about 2.5cm/1in). The square pattern is stronger than the diamond pattern. Folding trellises must be secured to a rigid framework. Plastic trellises are expensive but require no maintenance. An alternative to trellises or wires is wire-netting, which can be plastic-covered.

• **Archways of rustic timber.** Try making a pergola – series of linked arches.

• **A tripod of larch poles,** used to support climbers in a flower bed, thus giving height to the planting.

• **A colonnade** created by linking sturdy wooden posts with swags of rope, each side of a path.

• **Old tree stumps.** Cover them with scrambling plants if they are impossible to remove.

• **Old fruit trees** make good support for rampant scramblers such as roses or clematis. Place under the edge of the branch canopy rather than against the trunk, where there is more competition for food and water.

• **Good brickwork** will not be damaged by self-clinging plants such as ivy, though old mortar may be dislodged. To encourage sticking, paint the wall with diluted manure.

■ Eight climbers and wall shrubs for a shady wall

Cool, shady walls and fences, and indeed other structures in shady places, can be brightened up with these popular and easy-going plants.

• **Climbing hydrangea** (*Hydrangea petiolaris*) Deciduous climber which has flat heads of white flowers in summer. Self-supporting by aerial roots. At least 7.5m/25ft. No regular pruning needed. Likes moist soil. Takes a few years to settle in.

• **Cotoneaster** (*Cotoneaster horizontalis*) Deciduous wall shrub producing a system of flat, fishbone-like branches covered in autumn by red berries. Good autumn leaf colour. 2.4m/8ft. No regular pruning, any soil – good on chalky types.

• **Firethorn** (*Pyracantha varieties*) Evergreen wall shrub with masses of red, orange or yellow berries in autumn. Can attain 3.6m/12ft, but kept smaller by judicious pruning after flowering. Any soil.

• **Garrya** (*Garrya elliptica*) Evergreen wall shrub with greyish-green catkins in winter. 4m/12ft. Grows in any good fertile soil. No pruning. Best variety is 'James Roof'.

• **Ivy** (*Hedera*) Evergreen self-clinging climbers. Small-leaved, as in varieties of *H. helix*, plain green or variegated; or large as in the variegated *H. canariensis* 'Gloire de Marengo' and *H. colchica* 'Dentata Variegata'. Heights variable up to 10m/30ft. Prune hard in spring to prevent excessive bulk. Large-leaved varieties may be burned by frost in hard winters.

• **Ornamental quince** (*Chaenomeles speciosa*) Deciduous wall shrub with red, pink or white, saucer-shaped flowers in spring. To about 1.8m/6ft. Thin out old wood after flowering. Any well-drained soil.

• **Virginia creeper** (*Parthenocissus quinquefolia*) Grows very tall, but you can prune to desired height in winter. Deciduous, hand-shaped leaves turn brilliant scarlet and orange in autumn. Partially self-clinging by sucker pads: horizontal wires help. 15m/50ft. Any soil.

• **Winter jasmine** (*Jasminum nudiflorum*) Yellow flowers on bare stems in winter. About 3m/10ft. Any well-drained soil. After flowering, cut back old flowered shoots to 5cm/2in.

■ **Six climbers and wall shrubs for a sunny wall**

Suitable for a sunny, sheltered wall, or any structure which receives full sun.

• **Californian lilac** (*Ceanothus* species and varieties) Attractive wall shrubs, both evergreen and deciduous, producing mainly blue flowers in spring/early summer, or in summer and autumn. Height variable to 6m/20ft. Not suited to shallow, chalky soils; good drainage and shelter needed.

• **Chilean potato tree** (*Solanum crispum*) Vigorous semi-evergreen climber to 6m/20ft, with purplish blue, potato-like flowers in summer. 'Glasnevin' is a good variety. Shelter and good drainage needed. Prune previous year's shoots hard back in mid-spring.

• **Clematis** (*Clematis* species and hybrids) The large-flowered clematis, such as the purple *C. × jackmanii*, climb to about 3m/10ft. Most are summer-flowering. Other popular large-flowered hybrids: 'Nellie Moser' (pink with crimson stripe), 'Ernest Markham' (red), 'Hagley Hybrid' (deep pink), 'Lasurstern' (purplish), 'Mrs Cholmondeley' (pale blue), 'Perle d'Azur' (deep blue), 'The President' (bluish-purple) and 'Vyvyan Pennell' (violet-purple). These are all easy to grow. Easier still are the species clematis – such as *C. tangutica* (yellow flowers in autumn) and *C. montana* (spring, white 9m/30ft) and its variety 'Elizabeth' (pink). For pruning, see p57.

• **Honeysuckle** (*Lonicera periclymenum* 'Belgica') The early Dutch honeysuckle, with scented reddish-purple and yellowish flowers in early summer. Deciduous climber to 6m/20ft. Likes plenty of humus in soil. Thin out older stems in late winter.

• **Kolomikta vine** (*Actinidia kolomikta*) Deciduous climber with pink, white and green leaves, to 3.6m/12ft. Good for all kinds of supports. Prefers a rich acid or lime-free soil. Thin out if necessary in late winter. Allow a few years to settle in.

• **Wisteria** (*Wisteria floribunda* 'Macrobotrys') A sumptuous deciduous climber for all kinds of supports – lovely on a pergola. Very long trusses of lilac flowers tinted blue-purple in spring/early summer. 9m/28ft. Likes a rich moist soil. All growths should be cut back to within two or three buds of the main stems in late winter.

■ **Two climbers for quick screening**

These vigorous and fast-growing climbers are ideal for quickly covering tree stumps, unsightly sheds or garages, chain-link fencing, and so on.

• **Russian vine** (*Polygonum baldschuanicum*) Rampant deciduous climber which can grow at least 3m/10ft in a year and reach 12m/40ft, although you can cut back as necessary in late winter. Sprays of white flowers borne in great profusion midsummer to early autumn. Will grow in any soil.

• **Staff vine** (*Celastrus orbiculatus*) Deciduous climber to 9m/30ft. In autumn glows with brilliant orange and scarlet fruits, the foliage turning clear yellow. Any soil. If necessary, thin out and cut back in later winter.

■ **Four climbers for growing up trees**

Drab old trees benefit greatly from this treatment. Simply allow the climbers to twine through the trees at will – though in the early stages they may need guiding with bamboo canes. Do not plant too close to the trunk.

• *Clematis montana* This deciduous, very vigorous species can reach 12m/40ft. Masses of white cross-shaped flowers appear in spring. There are several pink varieties. Likes a good soil (but suitable for chalk) and its roots shaded.

• *Clematis tangutica* Grows up to 6m/20ft, so suitable for a small tree. Deciduous, with deep yellow lantern-shaped blooms in late summer and autumn. Conspicuous silver seed heads follow. Same conditions as *C. montana*.

• **Honeysuckle** (*Lonicera × americana*) A tall, vigorous hybrid honeysuckle with delicate, beautifully scented white flowers, ageing to ivory and yellow, in summer. 7m/23ft. Likes a moist fertile soil, also suitable for chalk.

• **Japanese crimson glory vine** (*Vitis coignetiae*) Very vigorous ornamental vine which can climb to 27m/90ft. The 30cm/ 12in-wide leaves turn brilliant scarlet and crimson in autumn before they fall. Likes a deep, rich, moist soil and plenty of sun. Good for house walls too.

Single Semi-double Double

Cluster Large-flowered

ROSES

Roses are the most romantic of all flowers, and among the most versatile. Many are deliciously scent-ed, and the blooms come in virtually every colour except blue, in spring, summer or autumn. Moreover, some roses offer the bonus in autumn of colourful fruits or hips.

You can grow small roses in tubs on the patio. Certain climbing varieties are ideal for brightening up a shady wall, and there are lots of climbers too for pergolas and similar supports and for climbing through trees. A recent fashion is for prostrate vari-eties used as groundcover – ideal for steep banks. Some roses are most suitable for shrub or mixed bor-ders, while the old-fashioned kinds are an inevitable choice for the cottage garden.

■ Eleven categories of roses

Terms such as "floribunda" and "hybrid tea" are still often heard but the traditional classification of roses has been superseded by a more logical system, which is followed in the description here.

• **Climbing roses** Do not climb in the true sense of the word – they have to be tied in to supports. They vary in height, but on average expect around 2.5–3.5m/8–12ft. There are various kinds: climbing varieties of large-flowered and cluster-flowered roses (see below); repeat-flowering climbers with several flushes of blooms during summer/autumn; and summer-flowering climbers with only one flush of blooms each year in the summer. Flowers of the last two kinds may be fully double, semi-double, or single (see diagram, p94).

• **Cluster-flowered roses** Previously known as floribunda roses. Flowers produced in large clusters throughout summer. Ideal for formal beds. These are bush roses, developing into bushes of quite regular outline. Heights vary from 45cm/18in to 1.8m/6ft, but the average is 0.9–1.2m/3–4ft.

• **Groundcover roses** Comparatively new group of roses with a prostrate or low-arching habit of growth. Flowers may be double, semi-double or single. Some varieties have only one flush of blooms in summer; others have several.

• **Hybrid musk roses** Types of shrub roses (see p96) developed early this century. The flower shape varies, but all hybrid musk roses are noted for superb scent. Blooms often produced well into autumn. Average height 1.5m/5ft.

• **Large-flowered roses** Previously known as hybrid tea roses. They are bush roses, developing into bushes of quite regular outline, growing on average to about 90cm/3ft; some varieties, however, attain 1.2–1.5m/4–5ft, while others do not exceed 60cm/2ft. All produce large individual flowers, perfectly shaped, often highly scented. Ideal for formal beds.

• **Miniature roses** There are no smaller roses than these – they attain no more than 45cm/18in in height, and many are very much shorter. The tiny blooms are scaled-down versions of large-flowered and cluster-flowered roses and are produced throughout the summer.

• **Old garden roses** The roses of the 19TH, 18TH and earlier centuries. Some groups are still popular today. BOURBONS have large, double, richly fragrant flowers which appear in several flushes throughout summer; 1.2–1.8m/4–6ft. MOSS ROSES have moss-like growths on the flower buds and stems, and the double blooms are usually highly fragrant; 1.2–1.8m/4–6ft. DAMASK ROSES have a highly distinctive fragrance, and the usually double blooms are produced over a long period; 1.2–1.8m/4–6ft.

• **Polyantha roses** Low-growing shrub roses which produce clusters of small double flowers during summer and into autumn. 30–90cm/1–3ft. Popular early this century.

• **Ramblers** Vigorous climbing roses which produce new growths from ground level each year. Many reach heights of 3.5–4.5m/12–15ft or more. Most carry clusters of double flowers in summer: one good, long display and then nothing more until next year.

• **Shrub roses** A very variable group, consisting mainly of quite large shrubs, 1.5–2.5m/5–8ft in height, with a similar spread. Recommended are the modern repeat-flowering shrub roses which produce several flushes of blooms during summer and into autumn. Other have only one flush in summer. Flowers may be single, semi-double or double.

• **Species roses** These are wild roses: shrubs which vary considerably in habit. Grown not only for attractive flowers, usually single, but often for colourful autumn hips or fruits, and sometimes for distinctive foliage or colourful thorns.

■ Five growing hints

Although they are thought to be difficult, roses need only a few basic requirements to succeed.

• **A well-drained soil is essential,** but it can be any type, from sand and chalk to clay, provided that it has lots of manure or garden compost worked in.

• **Full sun and shelter** are required for most roses if they are to grow and flower well.

• **Feed well** in spring and summer with a proprietary rose fertilizer. Keep well-watered in dry spells.

• **Serious pests and diseases** require vigorous campaigning. However, not all roses are prone to such problems: many shrub roses, in particular, are trouble-free.

• **Pruning** needs vary. Some roses – especially the large-flowered and cluster-flowered bush roses, and climbers and ramblers – require annual pruning for best results. Others need none, except to remove dead shoots. (See also p58.)

■ Five highly fragrant roses

All the plants listed here are exceptionally fragrant. All are bush roses, and must be pruned in spring. Remove all weak growth and reduce the remaining strong stems to 15–20cm/6–8in above ground level. These roses look best in formal beds, perhaps with an underplanting of prostrate groundcover plants for interest in winter and spring.

• **'Alec's Red'** Large-flowered rose with deep red blooms and a rich, sweet fragrance. Around 90cm/3ft. Disease-resistant.

• **'Elizabeth of Glamis'** Cluster-flowered bush rose with deep salmon-coloured blooms. 0.9–1.2m/3–4ft.

• **'Fragrant Cloud'** Large-flowered rose with scarlet blooms. About 90cm/3ft.

• **'Papa Meilland'** Large-flowered rose with velvety, deep crimson flowers. About 90cm/3ft. Treat against mildew.

• **'Scented Air'** Cluster-flowered rose with salmon-pink blooms. Can grow to at least 1.2m/4ft. Resists disease well.

■ Six roses for containers

These small-growing roses are especially recommended for growing in tubs on a patio. Containers measuring 30 x 30cm/12 x 12in are suitable for miniature roses, while 45 x 45cm/18 x 18in tubs are better for cluster-flowered and polyantha roses. Grow these plants in loam-based potting compost such as John Innes No. 2 or 3. Only the cluster-flowered varieties need regular pruning.

• **'Angela Rippon'** A miniature rose, no more than 30cm/12in high, and deservedly very popular. Small double flowers in a lovely shade of salmon-pink.

• **'Anna Ford'** This is a dwarf, cluster-flowered rose with a bushy spreading habit. About 45cm/18in. Masses of mandarin-red blooms, which later turn orange-red.

• **'Baby Masquerade'** A miniature, highly popular. It will not exceed much more than 30cm/12in. Bears yellow, pink and red flowers throughout the summer.

• **'Gentle Touch'** A miniature, 45cm/18in high. Pale pink formal blooms carried in large clusters, creating a great deal of colour in summer.

• **'Kerry Gold'** A low-growing, cluster-flowered rose. Not more then 45cm/18in. Deep golden-yellow blooms set against shiny, dark green foliage.

• **'Little White Pet'** An old polyantha rose, but still very popular and well worth growing. Attains 45cm/18in and freely produces masses of tiny white double blooms.

■ Three roses for shady walls

These modern repeat-flowering climbers, which bloom in summer and autumn, are suitable for growing against a cool, shady wall or fence, or other supports in the shade, such as pergolas or pillars. To prune, cut back the old side shoots to one or two buds in early spring.

• **'Aloha'** Large, coral-pink, double flowers freely produced. Grows to 2.4m/8ft.

• **'Golden Showers'** Highly popular variety with large, bright yellow flowers. About 2.4m/8ft.

• 'The New Dawn' A popular variety with the palest pink well-shaped blooms. A moderately vigorous grower, attaining about 3m/10ft.

■ Five repeat-flowering roses for growing up pillars or over pergolas

A succession of blooms during summer and autumn makes these roses ideal for training on pergolas, pillars or, indeed, sunny walls and fences. They look particularly lovely when large-flowered clematis are allowed to intertwine. Prune as Roses for Shady Walls (above).

• 'Altissimo' Large, single, velvety red flowers. Reaches a height of 4.5m/15ft.

• 'Compassion' In shape the flowers resemble those of large-flowered bush roses. They are scented and salmon in colour, shaded with orange. 3m/10ft.

• 'Parkdirektor Riggers' Single flowers in bright scarlet. Marvellous for training on a pillar – say, in a shrub border. About 2.4m/8ft.

• 'Pink Perpétue' A favourite, producing large clusters of bright pink flowers over a long period. 2.4m/8ft.

• 'Schoolgirl' Flowers shaped like those of large-flowered bush roses; well-scented and coppery apricot, flushed with pink. 3m/10ft.

■ Two roses for growing up trees

T hese very vigorous climbing roses will create a mass of flowers among the branches of large mature trees or high-lighted by conifers.

• *Rosa filipes* 'Kiftsgate' Vigorous climber, capable of attaining 9m/30ft. Produces huge clusters of small white flowers in mid-summer. Try it up a large, deep green conifer, such as Lawson cypress. Can actually outgrow smaller supports.

• *Rosa longicuspis* Grows to about 6m/20ft. Glossy, almost evergreen foliage and masses of small white flowers growing in trusses in early summer: if you can reach them, you'll find they have a fruity scent.

■ Four roses for groundcover

R oses with a prostrate or arching habit of growth are ideal for covering banks or the ground among shrubs. No pruning is needed.

• 'Grouse' Prostrate, with a spread of 3m/10ft. Produces masses of single, fragrant, pale pink blooms in summer. Shiny foliage. Plant 1.2m/4ft apart each way.

• **'Nozomi'** Prostrate habit, repeat-flowering. Small single blooms in large clusters, palest pink. Plant about 60cm/2ft apart each way for effective cover.

• **'Pheasant'** Prostrate habit with bold trusses of large flowers, deep rose pink and repeating. Plant 1.2m/4ft apart each way: it's quite vigorous.

• **'Red Bells'** An arching habit of growth. Large clusters of double blooms in brilliant crimson-red. Flowering period mid- or late summer. Plant 90cm/3ft apart each way.

■ Six roses for the shrub or mixed border

Owing to their more natural-looking habit of growth, these shrub roses make good companions for ornamental shrubs and hardy perennials. None of them needs regular pruning, and they are not too prone to diseases.

• **'Chinatown'** Repeat-flowering shrub rose of vigorous habit, to 1.8m/6ft, bearing flushes of deep yellow blooms.

• **'Fred Loads'** Repeat-flowering shrub rose with large, single, vivid orange-vermilion flowers. About 2.4m/8ft. Deservedly very popular.

• **'Frühlingsgold'** Summer-flowering shrub rose. To 2.4m/8ft. The huge, almost single blooms are creamy yellow and fragrant. Flowers early summer.

• **'Golden Wings'** Repeat-flowering shrub rose, tall and vigorous, about 2.4m/8ft. Large, single, well-scented, light golden-yellow blooms set against pale green foliage. Each flower has a "boss" of amber stamens.

• **Rosa moyesii** Marvellous dual-season shrub rose with brilliant red, single flowers in summer and large crops of bright, orange-red hips in autumn. Grows to about 2.4m/8ft.

• **Rosa rubrifolia** Species shrub rose with lots of interest: purplish-grey leaves carried on dark red stems; single pink flowers, large crops of brown-red hips in the autumn. Grows to about 2.4m/8ft.

■ Four roses for cottage gardens

Cottage and other country gardens call for old-fashioned shrub roses. Some of the most popular are listed here. None of them needs regular pruning.

• **'Mme Hardy'** A damask rose (one of the truly great varieties), with highly fragrant, double, pure white blooms in summer. About 1.5m/5ft.

• **'Mme Isaac Pereire'** A bourbon rose, repeat-flowering, growing to about 1.8m/6ft. Large purplish-crimson flowers are richly fragrant. Can be trained on a pillar if desired.

• **'Rosa Mundi'** Very popular rose with bright crimson and white striped flowers in early and mid-summer. A bushy shrub, about 1.2m/4ft. Watch it for mildew.

• **'William Lobb'** A moss rose, characterized by mossy growths on the buds and stalks. Summer-flowering, with flat crimson-purple blooms, very fragrant. Grows to 1.8m/6ft: it's best to support the stems.

■ Two standard roses

These are like small trees with a straight stem (about 90cm/3ft, or 1.5m/5ft in the case of weeping standards) and a head of branches at the top. They are useful for giving extra height in rose beds. The stems need to be permanently supported with a stout wooden stake. Many varieties are produced as standards by rose growers: here is just one shrub and one rambler. Many large-flowered and cluster-flowered varieties are also available as standards. Prune in the same way as bush roses, but cut all branches to the same length to form a perfectly symmetrical head.

• **'Canary Bird'** This shrub is often produced in standard form. Single bright yellow flowers in spring. Tolerates partial shade.

• **'Dorothy Perkins'** One of several rambler roses that are often produced as weeping standards. In this form it has an umbrella-shaped head of long pendulous branches. The flowers are rose-pink.

ROCK-GARDEN PLANTS

A rock garden need not be a miniature mountain range. Indeed, if your plot is a small one, a few well-shaped pieces of natural rock arranged as an attractive outcrop – perhaps on a bank, in a lawn or at one side of a garden pool – can make a perfect home for a little collection of alpines.

Choose a sunny spot with well-drained soil, and fill the spaces between the rocks with a good, gritty, loam-based potting compost, such as John Innes No. 1 with some extra grit added to it. You will need some flowering plants, some for foliage interest in autumn and winter, and some shrubby kinds for contrast in height and shape. Plant in autumn or spring, and afterwards cover the soil with a layer of stone chippings or pea shingle, which will help to suppress weeds and create a natural-looking effect.

■ Ten flowering rock-garden plants

Given good drainage and adequate sun, these will provide ample colour in spring and summer and need little attention, apart from trimming off dead flowers.

• *Campanula cochleariifolia* Very easily grown bellflower, with blue bell-like flowers freely produced from mid-summer to early autumn. 10–15cm/4–6in. Suitable for partial shade.

• **Candytuft** (*Iberis sempervirens*) Evergreen rock plant, about 20cm/8in high, with sheets of white flowers in spring and early summer. Grows well even in poor soils. Regularly remove dead flowers – then more blooms will follow.

• *Dianthus caesius* Known as the 'Cheddar Pink'. Grows to 15–30cm/6–12in and forms a mat of grey-green foliage. Pink fragrant flowers from late spring to mid-summer. Plenty of sun and good drainage. Ideal for chalky soils.

• *Geranium subcaulescens* One of the best rock-garden geraniums, flowering from spring to autumn. The blooms are crimson-magenta, each with a black "eye". 10–15cm/4–6in. Tolerates partial shade. Needs good drainage.

• **Gold dust** (*Alyssum saxatile*) Universally popular. In spring, a sheet of bright golden-yellow flowers, which contrast superbly with aubrieta. The grey-green leaves are evergreen. 20–30cm/8–12in. Cut plants back after flowering to keep compact. Likes plenty of sun.

• **Phlox** (*Phlox subulata*) Popular spreading mat-forming rock plant, which covers itself with starry flowers in spring. Shades of pink, purple, blue and red. About 10cm/4in but spreads to 45cm/18in. Likes fertile soil, and lots of sun.

• **Purple rock cress** (*Aubrieta deltoidea*) One of the most popular rock plants, with trailing or mat-forming habit and evergreen foliage. Plants smother themselves in spring with flowers in shades of red, purple, blue or pink. 5–8cm/2–3in. Likes sun and chalky soils. Cut back hard after flowering.

• **Saxifrage** (*Saxifraga* species/varieties) A huge group. Most form evergreen mats, hummocks or moss-like carpets of growth. In spring, studded with small rounded flowers in shades of red, pink, yellow or white, according to variety. 5–30cm/2in–1ft. Easiest to grow are varieties of Mossy, Kabschia and Engleria saxifrages, which like gritty soil, ideally containing chalk, and shade from the hottest sun.

• **Sun rose** (*Helianthemum nummularium*) Evergreen spreading prostrate plant, masses of single rose-like flowers in summer. Height 10–15cm/4–6in, spreads up to 60cm/2ft. Varieties in shades of red, orange, yellow and other colours. Needs plenty of sun and gritty soil. Can be cut back hard after flowering.

• **Thrift** (*Armeria maritima*) This is the common thrift, also known as sea thrift. Popular evergreen hummock-forming rock plant studded with pink globular flowers in spring and summer. 15–30cm/6–12in. Grow in full sun, well-drained soil. Remove dead flower heads.

■ Three foliage rock-garden plants

Their leaves give these plants an attractive appearance all the year round.

• **Houseleek** (*Sempervivum* species and varieties) A vast group, but all form rosettes of succulent leaves. Foliage colour includes many shades of green, often flushed with red or pink; and red or purple. 5–10cm/2–4in. Flowers produced in summer, but are not the main attraction. Will grow in the poorest soils, so long as drainage is good. Full sun needed.

• **Raoulia** (*Raoulia australis*) Forms completely prostrate mats of evergreen silvery foliage. Individual leaves are minute. Spreads to about 30cm/12in. Sole needs are gritty, well-drained soil and plenty of sun.

• **Stonecrop** (*Sedum spathulifolium*) Forms mats or hummocks of succulent greyish-green leaves flushed with red or purple. Yellow flowers in early summer. Variety 'Purpureum' is recommended, its leaves heavily flushed with purple. 5cm/2in. Likes same conditions as houseleeks (above).

■ Three rock-garden plants for shade

These plants, suitable for the cool, shady side of a rock garden, like moist soil conditions.

• *Campanula portenschlagiana* A vigorous bellflower forming a carpet of heart-shaped leaves, studded from early summer to well into autumn with deep blue bell-shaped flowers. Height 15cm/6in, spread 60cm/2ft.

• **Horned violet** (*Viola cornuta*) Large, lavender, violet-like flowers in summer. There are varieties in other colours. Height 15–30cm/6–12in. Remove dead flowers regularly.

• **Ramonda** (*Ramonda myconi*) Forms a rosette of evergreen, deep green leaves. Stems of lavender-blue, saucer-shaped flowers in spring. 8cm/3in. Needs a cool, shady aspect and should be planted in a vertical crevice. Likes a cool, moist peaty soil.

■ Five shrubs and conifers for the rock garden

A few shrubby plants, grown as specimens arranged here and there on the rock garden, will create attractive variations in height and form. They always look best sited on the lower levels – not perched at the top.

• *Cytisus × beanii* A broom. May grow to 90cm/3ft across, with a height of 45–60cm/1½–2ft. In spring and early summer, smothered with golden-yellow flowers. Thrives in poor, slightly acid soil, and needs full sun.

• **Dwarf mountain pine** (*Pinus mugo* varieties) Conifer forming a dome-shaped or rounded bush, with evergreen deep green "needles". Will attain about 60 x 60cm/2 x 2ft in 10 years. Grows well in chalky soil, but needs full sun and unpolluted air.

• *Genista lydia* Suitable for a large rock garden, this dwarf broom spreads to 1.8m/6ft and has a height of about 60cm/2ft. Arching greyish-green stems with narrow grey-green leaves carry bright yellow flowers in spring and early summer. Needs same conditions as *Cytisus* x *beanii*. (See p102)

• *Juniperus communis* 'Compressa' This juniper is one of the smallest conifers for the rock garden. Forms a tiny narrow column of evergreen, grey-green prickly foliage. Ultimate height 90cm/3ft, but only 30–45cm/12–18in after 10 years. Likes full sun; grows well in chalky soil.

• **Silver fir** (*Abies balsamea* 'Hudsonia') A compact dense bun-shaped conifer with evergreen, deep green, shiny foliage. A slow grower: 30cm/12in high after 10 years, ultimately 90cm/3ft. Easy and adaptable, but likes plenty of sun.

WATER PLANTS

Garden pools can look rather bleak unless you grace them with water plants. These should certainly include some waterlilies, with large, rounded, floating leaves which help to shade the water and exotic-looking blooms, mostly bowl-shaped, in summer and autumn.

Water plants are best planted during late spring or early summer. Most will be happy in ordinary fibrous garden soil in purpose-made planting baskets, but first you must line each basket with clean, coarse sacking. Before immersing in the pool, spread a layer of coarse gravel over the soil to prevent it from floating off and to prevent disturbance by fish. Baskets 25–30cm/10–12in square are suitable for most vigorous plants, but small versions, 20cm/8in square, are better for pygmy waterlilies and less invasive plants.

Baskets containing waterlilies should not be placed immediately on the bottom of the pool, but should be stood on bricks so that they are 15cm/6in below the water surface. Gradually lower them into their final positions as the plants grow.

■ Eight water plants for shallow water

The following are suitable for growing in a 23–30cm/ 9–12in depth of water. Most are marginal plants: in other words, plants for the shallow water at the pool edge.

• **Arrowhead** (*Sagittaria sagittifolia*) Marginal, 45–60cm / 1½–2ft tall, with broad, arrow-shaped, green leaves and pure white flowers with yellow centres, carried in sprays during summer. There is an even more attractive double-flowered form: 'Flore Pleno'.

• **Bog bean** (*Menyanthes trifoliata*) Marginal plant for the pond edge, which flowers in spring, with attractive fringed blooms, pinkish white in colour. Broad deep green leaves also attractive. 15–30cm/6–12in.

• **Flowering rush** (*Butomus umbellatus*) Not a true rush, but has rush-like leaves. Heads of bright pink flowers in summer and early autumn. A marginal, growing to about 1.2m/4ft. Vigorous, so use a large basket.

• **Marsh marigold** (*Caltha palustris* 'Plena') Highly popular marginal with double golden-yellow flowers in spring. About 15cm/6in. A small-growing plant for very shallow water. Remove any dying leaves in summer.

• **Pickerel weed** (*Pontederia cordata*) Vigorous: attains height of at least 60cm/2ft. Deep green, glossy, heart-shaped leaves and, in late summer and early autumn, spikes of blue flowers. One of the most exotic-looking water plants.

• **Water iris** (*Iris laevigata* and *I. pseudacorus*) Both have broad, sword-like leaves and typical iris flowers in early summer. The first grows to about 60cm/2ft and has deep blue flowers; the second attains 90–120cm/3–4ft and has striking yellow flowers. Both have variegated-leaved varieties. Remove the flower heads as they die to prolong flowering.

• **Water plantain** (*Alisma plantago-aquatica*) Forms clumps of large oval leaves and, in summer, loose spikes of pale lilac flowers. Quite vigorous: when in flower, can attain 90cm/3ft. Grows in very shallow water.

• **Waterlily** *Nymphaea laydekeri* varieties are the most suitable for shallow water. They include red 'Purpurata', carmine 'Lilacea' and pure white 'Alba'. Spread to 1m/3ft. All waterlilies need full sun and still water.

■ Three water plants for deep water

These plants are suitable for large pools with a water depth of 45–90cm/1–3ft. All are strong-growing and need large containers.

• **Golden club** (*Orontium aquaticum*) From tufts of long, wide, lush green leaves, conspicuous spikes of golden flowers appear in early summer. Easy to grow. Attains about 30cm/12in.

• **Water hawthorn** (*Aponogeton distachyus*) The long, oval, pale green leaves float on the water surface, like those of waterlilies. Spread to 1.2m/4ft. Waxy white flowers, beautifully scented, appear between early summer and autumn.

• **Waterlily** *Nymphaea marliacea* varieties are large vigorous waterlilies for big pools. Spread 2m/6ft or more. Best-known is 'Chromatella', with soft yellow flowers and deep olive-green leaves splashed with maroon.

■ Five water plants for tubs

Some of the small-growing water plants will be happy in a tub on the patio. Choose a container 60–90cm/2–3ft in diameter and depth, such as a half-barrel.

• **Arrowhead** (*Sagittaria sagittifolia*) See p103.

• **Bog bean** (*Menyanthes trifoliata*) See p104.

• **Marsh marigold** (*Caltha palustris* 'Plena') See p104.

• **Waterlily** *Nymphaea pygmaea* varieties are miniature or pygmy waterlilies which grow in as little as 15cm/6in of water, spreading to no more than 30cm/12in. Tiny flowers in summer and into autumn. 'Alba' is white, 'Helvola' canary yellow.

• **Whorled milfoil** (*Myriophyllum verticillatum*) See p106.

■ Three plants for the bog garden

You can create a bog garden at the edge of a pool, where the soil is kept permanently moist by overflowing water. To achieve this artificially, extend a pool liner under a marginal band of soil. All plants listed need moist soil, but don't like to actually stand in water.

• **Astilbe** (*Astilbe* × *arendsii*) Clumps of deeply cut foliage, often flushed with copper. In summer striking feathery plumes of flowers appear. Many varieties, shades of red, pink, also white. 60–90cm/2–3ft. Lift and divide every 3–4 years. Herbaceous habit.

• **Iris** (*Iris kaempferi* and *I. sibirica*) Long sword-like leaves, and flowers in early summer. First grows 90cm/3ft high; flower colours include blue, reddish-purple, lavender, pink and white. Second, of similar height, available as hybrids in shades of blue, pink or white. Lift and divide every 4 to 5 years. *I. kaempferi* needs lime-free soil.

• **Primula** The many bog or moisture-loving primulas include: *P. denticulata*, lilac or purple; the dwarf *P. rosea*, bright rose-pink; *P. aurantiaca*, yellow-orange; *P. japonica*, magenta-red; *P. burmanica*, deep rose-purple; *P. pulverulenta*, crimson; *P. bulleyana*, light orange; and *P. florindae*, pale yellow. Heights vary widely, from 15cm/6in to 1m/3ft. Sometimes they self-sow. Lift and divide if they become overcrowded.

■ Four plants to aerate the water

Submerged water plants, which produce oxygen beneficial to fish and other pond life, are essential for the health of a pool. However not all are decorative, and they can get out of hand. They are usually supplied in bunches of unrooted cuttings. Plant at the rate of one small bunch for every 0.2–0.3 sq m/2–3sq ft of the pool's surface area. Divide in autumn if they outgrow their space.

• **Common fish weed** (*Lagarosiphon major*) Produces dark green, thick, snake-like growths. Excellent oxygenator. A strong grower. Almost evergreen.

• **Water crowfoot** (*Ranunculus aquatilis*) Deep green floating foliage (rather clover-like) and deeply cut underwater foliage. Bright white and yellow flowers appear among the floating leaves in summer.

• **Water violet** (*Hottonia palustris*) In spring, pale lilac blooms appear on thin stems growing well above the water and surrounded by light green, finely cut foliage.

• **Whorled milfoil** (*Myriophyllum verticillatum*) Feathery foliage arranged in whorls around the stems.

TREES AND SHRUBS

The main framework of most planting schemes is provided by trees and shrubs (including conifers). They evoke permanence, and quick-growing kinds will soon give an air of maturity to a new garden. There are trees and shrubs to supply colour and character for every season, and for "difficult" situations.

Most types are labour-saving, in that they do not need regular pruning. However, some of the most popular, such as forsythia, do need pruning annually to ensure a good flower display the following year. Provided that they have suitable conditions, trees and shrubs are easy-going, but like all garden plants they appreciate good treatment: feed in spring, water in dry spells, mulch to keep the soil moist and weeds down. Few species are plagued by pests and diseases. (Unless otherwise stated, heights given in following lists are those to be expected after 20 years: ultimate heights vary according to growing conditions.)

■ Twelve trees and shrubs for lawn specimens

Some types are so distinctive that they are best planted in isolation. When planting in a lawn, leave a 45cm/18in radius of bare soil around each one, as grass right up to the stems or trunks retards growth.

• **Birch** (*Betula pendula* 'Youngii') A weeping form, with a white trunk and a mushroom-shaped head of branches which eventually reach the ground. Deciduous 4.5–6m/15–20ft. Any soil. Sun or partial shade.

• **Brewer's weeping spruce** (*Picea brewerana*) Dramatic evergreen conifer shaped rather like a Japanese pagoda. Foliage is deep green. 7.5m/25ft. Likes a good, deep, moist soil, ideally acid. Full sun or partial shade. Needs time to establish and look good.

• **Cherry** (*Prunus* x *hillieri* 'Spire') Ornamental cherry with a narrow columnar habit – ideal for limited space. Soft pink blossom in spring. Good autumn leaf colours. Any fertile soil, plenty of sun. 4.5–6m/15–20ft.

• **Golden Irish yew** (*Taxus baccata* 'Fastigiata Aurea') Conifer, forming a narrow column of yellow-green evergreen foliage. 3.6–4.5m/12–15ft. Needs full sun for best colour. Any soil suitable, including chalk.

• **Holly** (*Ilex aquifolium* 'Argentea Pendula') Weeping evergreen holly with white-edged leaves and crops of red berries in winter. 4.5–6m/15–20ft. Suitable for any soil, including chalk. Flourishes in sun or partial shade.

• **Irish juniper** (*Juniperus communis* 'Hibernica') Evergreen conifer, forming a narrow column of prickly grey-green foliage. 4.5–6m/15–20ft. Chalky soils, likes full sun.

• **Japanese cherry** (*Prunus* 'Amanogawa') Deciduous tree, upright, good for limited space. Draped in spring with fragrant, semi-double, pale pink blossoms. 4.5–6m/15–20ft. Any good, well-drained soil and plenty of sun.

• **Japanese cherry** (*Prunus* 'Kiku-shidare Sakura') Beautiful weeping cherry, wreathed with double, deep pink blossoms in spring. 4.5–6m/15–20ft. Deciduous. Any fertile, well-drained soil, plenty of sun.

• **Juniper** (*Juniperus virginiana* 'Skyrocket') Evergreen conifer forming a narrow column, excellent for small gardens. Foliage is bluish grey. 4.5–6m/15–20ft. Grows well in chalky soils; sun or partial shade.

• **Maidenhair tree** (*Ginkgo biloba*) Pyramid-shaped deciduous tree. Fan-shaped, light green leaves turn deep yellow in autumn. 9m/30ft. Best in sheltered sunny spot; any ordinary, humus-rich soil.

• **Weeping spring cherry** (*Prunus subhirtella* 'Pendula Rosea') Deciduous. Mushroom-shaped head of branches eventually touches the ground. The early spring blossoms are pale pink, emerging from deep pink buds. 3–4.5m/10–15ft. Any fertile, well-drained soil in sun or partial shade.

• **Willow-leaved pear** (*Pyrus salicifolia* 'Pendula'). Small weeping tree, deciduous, willow-like silvery leaves. 4.5–6m/15–20ft. Any good well-drained soil in sun or partial shade.

■ Twelve shrubs for winter colour

Every garden should have a few shrubs for winter colour. The following offer colour from flowers, foliage or bark. Try combining each of these features to create an attractive mixed group.

• **Cornelian cherry** (*Cornus mas*) Masses of small yellow flowers appear on the bare branches of this excellent shrub. 3–3.6m/10–12ft. Likes a good fertile soil and plenty of sun.

• **Dogwood** (*Cornus alba* 'Sibirica') Deciduous shrub producing thickets of brilliant red stems. Cut down almost to the ground each year in early spring. Likes a moist soil, and sun or partial shade. Height of annual stems about 1.8m/6ft.

• **Elaeagnus** (*Elaeagnus pungens* 'Maculata') Evergreen shrub with brilliant gold-splashed leaves which really show up in winter sunshine. 2.4–3.6m/8–12ft. Any ordinary soil, including chalk. Sun or partial shade.

• **Laurustinus** (*Viburnam tinus* 'Eve Price') Evergreen shrub with deep green foliage and flat heads of white pink-tinted flowers from bright pink buds. Flowers from late autumn to early spring. Reaches 2.4–3m/8–10ft. Will thrive in any good soil, also chalky types. Full sun or partial shade.

• **Mahonia** (*Mahonia japonica*) Evergreen, with large, deep green, compound leaves, and long sprays of scented yellow flowers. 2m/6ft. Any good moist soil, in sun or partial shade.

• **Mezereon** (*Daphne mezereum*) Neat deciduous bush soon reaching about 1.5m/5ft. Produces clusters of scented purple-red flowers in late winter. Excellent on chalky soils. Sun or partial shade.

• ***Rhododendron*** ('Praecox') Semi-evergreen, small shrub with funnel-shaped, rose-purple flowers unusually early, in late winter or early spring. 120–150cm/4–5ft. Must be grown in lime-free soil; preferably dappled shade.

• **Sawara cypress** (*Chamaecyparis pisifera* 'Boulevard') Broad, cone-shaped, evergreen conifer, with silvery blue foliage which shows up well in winter. About 2.4m/8ft. Needs moist soil, not happy in chalky or clay soils. Open sunny position is best.

• **Viburnum** (*Viburnum farreri*) Deciduous shrub producing clusters of beautifully scented white blooms tinted with pink, late autumn, to early spring. 2.4–3.6m/8–12ft. Any fertile, moist, humus-rich soil. Full sun or partial shade.

• **White cedar** (*Thuja occidentalis* 'Rheingold') Evergreen conifer forming a broad cone or dome shape. Foliage is coppery gold, turning a deep gold in summer; dramatic in winter when orange-tinted. 1.8–2.4m/6–8ft. Any ordinary garden soil, but full sun for best colour.

• **Willow** (*Salix alba* 'Chermesina') Forms thickets of stems, to about 2.4m/8ft, if cut down almost to ground level in early spring each year; otherwise becomes a huge tree for a large garden. These young stems are brilliant orange-scarlet. Likes any moist soil, and sun or partial shade.

• **Witch hazel** (*Hamamelis mollis* 'Pallida') Deciduous shrub with masses of spidery, pale yellow scented flowers. Height at least 2.4m/8ft. Prefers acid or neutral soil, moist and rich in humus, but will tolerate enriched chalky soil. Sheltered spot in sun or partial shade.

■ Ten shrubs for spring colour

These flowering shrubs are indispensable for bright colour in the spring garden. Grow some spring-flowering bulbs around them, to augment the effect.

• **Barberry** (*Berberis darwinii*) Highly popular evergreen shrub with shiny, deep green, holly-like leaves and deep yellow flowers followed by blackish berries. Any soil, including chalk. Sun or partial shade. Grows to around 2.4m/8ft.

• **Broom** (*Cytisus scoparius* hybrids) Green stems bear masses of yellow, red, cream or white flowers. Height about 2.4m/8ft, very quickly attained. Good for poor, sandy, acid soils, needs full sun. Cut off dead flower heads.

• **Californian lilac** (*Ceanothus* 'Delight') Evergreen shrub which smothers itself with bright blue flowers. At least 3m/10ft. Likes a light fertile soil, and a sheltered position in full sun.

• **Flowering currant** (*Ribes sanguineum* varieties) Popular deciduous shrub flowering in long pendulous trusses in early spring. Several varieties, in shades of red or pink; there is also a white variety. Any soil; sun or partial shade. Thin out some of the oldest wood in spring. 1.8–2.4m/6–8ft, quickly attained.

• **Forsythia** (*Forsythia*) Seen in almost every garden, this deciduous shrub is wreathed with large golden-yellow flowers. Around 2.4m/8ft, quickly attained. Any soil; sun or partial shade. Cutting back old flowered stems immediately after flowering keeps the tree in shape and encourages a good show of flowers. 'Lynwood' is especially popular and free-flowering.

• **Jew's mallow** (*Kerria japonica* 'Pleniflora') Deciduous shrub with green stems, studded in spring with double golden-yellow flowers. Quickly reaches about 2.4m/8ft. Any soil; sun or partial shade. Cut back old flowered stems to new shoots, immediately after flowering.

• **Lilac** (*Syringa vulgaris* varieties) Large upright trusses of fragrant flowers appear in late spring. Many varieties in shades of red, pink, purple, blue, cream and white. 2.4–3.6m/8–12ft. Any soil; sun or partial shade. Cut off dead flower heads.

• **Magnolia** (*Magnolia* × *soulangiana*) Deciduous shrub with huge goblet-shaped flowers, white flushed with purple, before the leaves. 3–4.5m/10–15ft. Likes a fertile soil (preferably acid), and a sheltered spot in sun or partial shade.

• **Ornamental quince** (*Chaenomeles* × *superba*) Deciduous shrub with large flowers like single roses, in shades of red, pink or orange-scarlet. Brilliant red 'Fire Dance' is a good variety. 1.5m/5ft. Any soil in sun or partial shade. Thin out if necessary after flowering.

• **Snowy mespilus** (*Amelanchier canadensis*) This deciduous suckering shrub has a mass of white starry flowers in spring. In autumn the leaves take on brilliant clear red tints before they fall, especially in acid soil. 2.4–3m/8–10ft. Likes a fertile, moist soil in sun or partial shade.

■ Fifteen shrubs for summer colour

Arepertoire for reliable and easy shrubs to grow for their flowers or coloured foliage. Some of these should be in every shrub or mixed border.

• **Abelia** (*Abelia* × *grandiflora*) Bushy semi-evergreen which produces its tubular pink and white flowers from mid-summer to mid-autumn. 1.5–1.8m/5–6ft, soon attained. Needs a warm, sunny sheltered spot and well-drained soil.

• **Barberry** (*Berberis* × *ottawensis* 'Purpurea') Vigorous shrub grown for its large oval, rich red-purple foliage. Quickly attains 2.4–3.6m/8–12ft. Grows on any soil, particularly good on chalk, and best in full sun.

• **Butterfly bush** (*Buddleia davidii* varieties) Highly popular deciduous shrub, producing long, thick spikes of flowers in late summer and autumn, which attract butterflies. Colours include shades of red, purple, blue, pink and white. Best to cut hard back in early spring each year, when new shoots can reach a height of 1.8–2.4m/6–8ft. Lovely honey-like scent. Any soil, good on chalk, full sun.

• **Deutzia** (*Deutzia* hybrids) Bushy deciduous shrubs with masses of starry flowers over a long period. Varieties come in pink, purple or white shades. 1.2–1.8m/4–6ft, quickly achieved. Any well-drained soil in a sunny spot or dappled shade. Cut out old flowered stems immediately after flowering.

• **Dogwood** (*Cornus kousa chinensis*) Bushy spreading shrub with four-petalled white flowers in early summer. Leaves turn crimson in autumn before they fall. At least 3m/10ft. Likes a fertile soil and full sun.

• **Escallonia** (*Escallonia* hybrids) Bushy evergreen shrubs, ideal for coastal gardens. Inland, they need a sheltered site. Provide full sun and well-drained soil – good on chalk. Many varieties, with masses of flowers in shades of red, pink or white. 1.5–2.4m/5–8ft, soon attained.

• *Fuchsia magellanica* Another good seaside shrub, with a long succession of crimson and purple bell-like flowers.

Deciduous. Can quickly attain 1.2–1.8m/4–6ft. Needs well-drained but humus-rich soil and plenty of sun. In cold areas stems may be killed by frost – in which case prune hard back.

• **Golden mock orange** (*Philadelphus coronarius* 'Aureus') There is no finer gold-leaved deciduous shrub. For best colour grow in partial shade. Will reach about 1.8m/8ft in a few years. Any soil, good on chalk. Prune back old flowered stems immediately after flowering.

• **Hibiscus** (*Hibiscus syriacus*) Bushy deciduous shrub producing large cup-shaped flowers in summer and autumn. Many varieties in shades of red, pink, purple, blue and white. 3m/10ft. Likes a rich, well-drained soil and a sheltered spot in full sun.

• **Shrubby cinquefoil** (*Potentilla fruticosa* varieties) These have the longest flowering period of any shrub. Flowers resemble single roses, in shades of yellow, orange, red, pink, cream and white. Heights vary from 60–120cm/2–4ft quickly attained. Good for hot, dry spots. Trim over lightly after flowering.

• **Shrubby veronica** (*Hebe* x *franciscana* 'Blue Gem') Bushy evergreen shrub with a long succession of violet-blue flowers in spikes. 1.2m/4ft, quickly attained. Needs a warm sheltered spot in full sun, with well-drained soil. Good chalk. Trim off dead flowers.

• **Smoke tree** (*Cotinus coggygria* 'Foliis Purpureis') One of the best deciduous shrubs for purple foliage. Leaves turn light red in autumn. About 3.6m/12ft. Any well-drained soil in sun or partial shade.

• **Snowball tree** (*Viburnum opulus* 'Sterile') Large round heads of white flowers, like snowballs. A large vigorous shrub: at least 3.6m/12ft. Any soil, good on chalk, sun or partial shade. Watch out for blackfly in summer.

• **Sun rose** (*Cistus* 'Silver Pink') One of the hardiest sun roses. An evergreen bush with large silvery pink flowers like single roses. Soon reaches 60–90cm/2–3ft. Ideal for a hot, dry spot.

• **Weigela** (*Weigela* hybrids) Easily grown deciduous shrubs producing masses of pink, red or white funnel-shaped flowers in early summer. Quickly grows to 1.5–1.8m/5–6ft. Any soil in sun or partial shade. Cut back old flowered shoots to new ones lower down, immediately after flowering.

■ Ten shrubs for autumn colour

An autumn garden can be highly colourful if it includes some of these shrubs. Some are grown for their autumn leaf colour and/or berries, others for their flowers. To complement them, plant some autumn-flowering bulbs and perennials, such as autumn crocuses and Michaelmas daisies.

• **Barberry** (*Berberis thunbergii*) Leaves turn brilliant red in autumn, when there are also large crops of small red berries. At least 120cm/4ft, quickly attained. Any well-drained soil; good on chalk. Full sun or partial shade.

• **Californian lilac** (*Caenothus* 'Gloire de Versailles') Starts flowering in summer and continues well into autumn. Deciduous, with masses of scented light powder-blue flowers. 1.5m/5ft. Likes a light fertile soil and a sheltered position in full sun. Prune hard back in early spring.

• *Caryopteris* **x** *clandonensis* Dwarf shrub, about 60cm/2ft in height, with aromatic greyish-green leaves and a long succession of blue flowers. Needs plenty of sun. Any soil. Cut hard back in early spring.

• *Cotoneaster* '**Cornubia**' Large semi-evergreen shrub, whose branches are weighed down in autumn and winter by tremendous crops of red berries. Height around 6m/20ft. For any soil, including chalk, and sun or partial shade.

• **Firethorn** (*Pyracantha coccinea* 'Lalandei') Evergreen shrub completely covered with orange-red berries in autumn. 3–3.6m/10–12ft, quickly attained. Grows anywhere, in sun or partial shade.

• **Japanese maple** (*Acer palmatum*) Varieties grown for their brilliant autumn leaf colour – generally flame-coloured. Very slow growing, 2.4–3.6m/8–12ft. Ideal for dappled shade of woodland. Needs shelter. Likes cool, moist, humus-rich soil.

• **Sea buckthorn** (*Hippophae rhamnoides*) Plant both male and female plants for huge crops of bright orange berries in autumn. Attractive deciduous silvery foliage. 2.4–3m/8–10ft. Excellent for seaside gardens. Sun or partial shade.

• **Smoke tree** (*Cotinus coggygria* 'Flame') Rounded shrub with the most brilliant orange autumn leaf colour. Plumes of pink flowers in summer, fading to a smokey grey. At least 2.4m/8ft. Any well-drained soil in full sun.

• **Spindle** (*Euonymus europaeus* 'Red Cascade') Bears an incredibly large crop of brilliant red and orange fruits. Good autumn leaf colour. 2.4–3m/8–10ft. Any soil; good on chalk. Sun or partial shade.

• **Stag's horn sumach** (*Rhus typhina*) Interesting shrub with antler-like branches and large compound leaves, which turn to brilliant shades of red and orange in autumn. Suckers freely. 3–4.5m/10–15ft. Any soil, and sun or partial shade.

■ Three shrubs with highly fragrant flowers

Plant these shrubs near a door, path or patio where their powerful scent can be fully appreciated. Choose a wind-free spot close to the house if possible, so that the scent is even more pronounced.

• *Daphne* x *burkwoodii* Semi-evergreen shrub with pale pink flowers, in large clusters, in late spring and early summer. Try to obtain the variety 'Somerset'. 1.2m/4ft. Any soil, including chalk; sun or partial shade.

• **Mexican orange blossom** (*Choisya ternata*) Neat bushy evergreen with shiny leaves, and a long succession (spring to autumn) of white flowers, which resemble orange blossom. Prune after flowering. Soon attains 1.8m/6ft. Choose a warm sheltered spot in full sun.

• **Mock orange** (*Philadelphus* hybrids) Popular deciduous shrubs with large white flowers in early summer, smelling of orange blossom. 1.8–3.6m/6–12ft, quickly attained. Any soil, good on chalk, and full sun or partial shade. Cut back old flowered shoots after flowering.

■ Six shrubs for shade with dry soil

Dense shade under large trees, where the soil dries out in summer, is a difficult situation for plants, yet the following will flourish. Dig in plenty of organic matter before planting, and water well in summer.

• **Cherry laurel** (*prunus laurocerasus* 'Otto Luyken') A dwarf shrub, about 60cm/2ft high, with long narrow shiny evergreen leaves and, in spring, spikes of white flowers. Makes excellent dense groundcover.

• **Holly** (*llex aquifolium* 'J.C. van Tol') Many hollies are suitable for shade with dry soil, but this variety bears particularly heavy crops of red berries. 6m/20ft. The evergreen leaves are almost spineless.

• **Oregon grape** (*Mahonia aquifolium*) Vigorous suckering shrub with evergreen compound leaves and, in spring, clusters of scented yellow flowers, followed by blue-black berries. Excellent groundcover shrub. Can be pruned hard back each spring, otherwise it attains 90–120cm/3–4ft.

• **Skimmia** (*Skimmia reevesiana*) Small, evergreen, rounded shrub with white flowers in spring, followed by red berries. 60–90cm/2–3ft. Excellent groundcover shrub. Dislikes chalky soils. *Skimmia japonica* tolerates any soil type.

• **Snowberry** (*Symphoricarpos rivularis*) Forms dense thickets of stems and bears huge clusters of large, white, marble-like berries. Grows in the poorest soils. Quickly attains 1.8m/6ft.

• **Spotted laurel** (*Aucuba japonica* 'Crotonifolia') Rounded evergreen shrub with large, evergreen, laurel-like leaves heavily speckled with gold. 1.8–2.4m/6–8ft.

■ Six shrubs for shade with moist soil

Many choice shrubs thrive in the dappled shade cast by trees, provided that the soil remains moist and does not dry out in summer. They like plenty of peat or leafmould worked into the soil before planting, and appreciate a mulch of these materials.

• **Azalea, deciduous** Large clusters of trumpet-shaped or honeysuckle-like flowers in late spring/early summer. Various groups, such as the Ghent and Knap Hill hybrids, with flowers in a wide range of strong and pastel colours (including yellows, reds, oranges and pinks). 1.8–2.4m/6–8ft. Lime-free soil essential.

• **Azalea, evergreen** The Kurume hybrids are dwarf spreading plants, about 60–90cm/2–3ft high, which smother themselves with small starry flowers in late spring. Colours include shades of red, pink and purple. Lime-free soil essential.

• **Camellia** (*Camellia* varieties) Evergreen shrubs with handsome glossy foliage, flowering in winter or spring, with large double or single flowers in shades of pink, red and white. Hundreds of varieties: most popular are varieties of *C. japonica* and *C.* x *williamsii*. 1–4m/3–13ft. Lime-free soil essential. Avoid a position that receives early morning sun, or frosted flowers may burn owing to rapid thawing.

• **Fig-leaf palm** (*Fatsia japonica*) Evergreen shrub with huge, shiny, hand-shaped leaves, and massive heads of white flowers in autumn. 2.4–3.6m/8–12ft. Likes a sheltered position.

• **Hydrangea** (*Hydrangea macrophylla*) There are two types: those with large mop-like heads of flowers, and others with flat heads. The former have flowers in shades of red, pink or blue. The latter have mainly blue or blue and white flowers. Pink or red hydrangeas become blue if the soil is acid. 1.5–2m/5–6ft. Cut off dead flower heads in early spring.

• **Rhododendron** (hardy hybrids) There is a vast range of rhododendrons, but the hardy hybrids are very reliable in all parts of Britain, are easy to grow and flower freely in spring. Dozens of varieties, with large clusters of flowers in shades of pink, red, purple and other colours. 30cm–6m/1–20ft. All are evergreen. Pick off seed heads. Lime-free soil essential.

■ Five popular flowering trees

These are widely planted small trees which you could include in a shrub border to give extra height; or, if you prefer you could use them as isolated specimens, although none of them has a particularly distinctive shape.

• **Autumn cherry** (*Prunus subhirtella* 'Autumnalis') An extremely useful deciduous tree for winter interest, as the small, semi-double, white flowers are produced, on and off, between late autumn and early spring. 6m/20ft. Any fertile soil is suitable. Sun or partial shade.

• **Crab apple** (*Malus floribunda*) Popular and beautiful deciduous spring-flowering tree. The arching branches bear masses of white flowers, from red buds. Later, small yellow and red fruits appear. About 4.5m/15ft. Sun or partial shade, fertile soil.

• **Golden rain** (*Laburnum* x *watereri* 'Vossii') The ubiquitous laburnum is a fountain of golden flowers in late spring/early summer, and then sadly not of great interest for the rest of the year. However, it grows anywhere. 4.5m/15ft, deciduous.

• **Japanese cherry** (*Prunus* 'Kanzan') Undoubtedly the most popular of the many Japanese cherries. Laden in spring with double purplish–pink blossoms. However, like the golden rain, it is not particularly interesting for 50 weeks of the year! Both can support clematis for later colour. Likes a good fertile soil and plenty of sun. About 7.5m/25ft, deciduous.

• **Thorn** (*Crataegus oxyacantha* 'Paul's Scarlet') Mass of double scarlet flowers in late spring makes this one of the most popular of the thorns. The attractive, red "haws" last well into winter; leaves colour well in autumn. Rounded head. 4.5–6m/15–20ft. Deciduous. Likes an open sunny spot; thrives in any soil. A good flowering tree for an exposed windy garden.

■ Eight trees for foliage colour

ere is a selection of superb trees with summer, autumn or winter foliage colour. They can be grown on their own, or in a shrub or mixed border.

• **Box elder** (*Acer negundo* 'Variegatum') With green leaves conspicuously edged with white, giving a very light effect overall. About 6m/20ft. Any good soil; sun or partial shade.

• **Crab apple** (*Malus tschonoskii*) Brilliant red and orange autumn leaf colour. A neat cone-shaped tree, height about 9m/30ft. Any fertile soil; sun or partial shade.

• **Golden false acacia** (*Robinia pseudoacacia* 'Frisia') Very popular deciduous tree with golden-yellow foliage from spring to autumn. About 7.5m/25ft. Needs plenty of sun, but suitable for any well-drained soil.

• **Golden honey locust** (*Gleditsia triacanthos* 'Sunburst') Deciduous tree, whose young foliage is bright yellow, becoming lime green. 7.5m/25ft. Any soil in full sun.

• **Koster's blue spruce** (*Picea pungens* 'Koster') Broad, cone-shaped, evergreen conifer with silvery blue foliage all year round – but shows up particularly well in winter. 7.5m/25ft. Likes a sunny position; thrives in any soil.

• **Monterey cypress** (*Cupressus macrocarpa* 'Goldcrest') Cone-shaped conifer which will attain around 9m/30ft. Brilliant golden-yellow foliage, particularly eye-catching in winter. Needs full sun. Any soil. Best growth in mild seaside gardens.

• **Purple-leaved plum** (*Prunus cerasifera* 'Pissardii') Highly popular round-headed deciduous tree. Deep red young foliage turns deep purple. White flowers in spring. 6m/20ft. Any soil. Sun or partial shade.

• **Thorn** (*Crataegus prunifolia*) Deciduous round-headed tree with brilliant scarlet and orange autumn foliage, and red berries. White flowers in early summer. 4.5–6m/15–20ft; can also be cut back and grown as a hedge. Likes an open sunny spot; any soil. Good for exposed windy gardens.

■ Three trees with colourful fruits

The following are particularly noted for their heavy crops of colourful autumn fruits or berries.

• **Crab apple** (*Malus* 'Golden Hornet') Huge crops of large, bright, yellow crab apples which last well into winter, after the leaves have fallen. 5.5m/18ft. Any good fertile soil in sun or partial shade.

• **Mountain ash** (*Sorbus* 'Joseph Rock') Upright compact tree with large clusters of cream-yellow berries in autumn. Also superb autumn leaf colour. 6m/20ft. Any ordinary garden soil, sun or partial shade.

• **Mountain ash** (*Sorbus aucuparia* 'Fastgiata') A narrow upright tree, far better for small gardens than the species mountain ash. Large crops of orange-red berries in autumn. Handsome deep green foliage, deciduous. About 6m/20ft. Any ordinary garden soil in sun or partial shade.

■ Three trees with colourful bark

Some trees have the most beautiful bark, which shows up particularly well in the winter garden. Ideally, you should use the following as isolated specimens.

• **Birch** (*Betula ermanii*) A large deciduous tree, with peeling creamy-white bark, tinted with pink. The branches are orange-brown. 6–7.5m/20–25ft. Likes a sheltered position in sun or partial shade. Any good garden soil.

• **Cherry** (*Prunus serrula*) A small round-headed deciduous tree with beautiful, glossy, reddish-brown peeling bark. In mid-spring produces small white blossoms. 6–7.5m/20–25ft. Any good fertile garden soil in sun or partial shade.

• **Paper-bark maple** (*Acer griseum*) This also has peeling bark, thin and papery, revealing new reddish-brown bark underneath. Leaves turn to flame shades in autumn before they fall.

Height 4.5m/15ft. Likes a sheltered spot in sun or partial shade; any moist fertile soil.

GROUNDCOVER

Certain ornamental plants will provide a low canopy of foliage sufficiently dense to prevent weeds from establishing beneath it. These are known as ground-cover plants. They enable you to keep a garden look-ing neat even if you lack the time or inclination for routine maintenance such as weeding and mowing. For example, they offer a labour-saving alternative to large areas of grass, or a way to reduce weeding between shrubs and roses. They will not suppress perennial weeds such as docks, nettles, bracken, couch grass and ground elder, so you must eradicate these before planting by spraying them when they are in full growth in spring and summer with a weedkiller containing glyphosate.

To get groundcover plants off to the best possible start, prepare the ground well by adding bulky organic matter, such as well-rotted farmyard manure or gar-den compost, and applying a dressing of blood, bone and fishmeal fertilizer.

■ Five groundcover plants for steep banks

An obvious problem site that benefits from groundcover is a steep bank: certainly this could be grassed, but it would be difficult to mow, and in any case groundcover plants provide a more colourful and interesting solution. If your bank is large enough, you can mix the following plants.

• *Cotoneaster microphyllus* This cotoneaster reaches 30–45cm/12–18in and has dense mounded growth, tiny ever-green leaves and red berries. Choose a sunny or lightly shaded site. Any soil. Planting distance: 45–60cm/1½–2ft.

• *Euonymus fortunei* 'Emerald 'n' Gold' A woody carpeting evergreen, 23cm/9in high, providing dense cover in sun or shade. Small dark green leaves edged with bright yellow. Any well-drained soil will be suitable. Planting distance: 30–45cm/12–18in.

• *Juniperus horizontalis* Prostrate evergreen carpeting conifer. A good variety is 'Bar Harbour' with greyish-green foliage. Best in full sun on well-drained soil; particularly good on chalk. Planting distance: 45–60cm/1½–2ft.

• **Lesser periwinkle** (*Vinca minor*) Evergreen carpeting plant with starry blue, white or purple flowers in spring. 10–15cm/4–6in. Tolerates deep shade, full sun and any soil (except poorly drained). Planting distance: 38–45cm/15–18in (less on very poor soils).

• **St John's wort** (*Hypericum calycinum*) Low-growing shrub
that spreads to form a matted carpet of leafy suckering
growths. Large bright yellow flowers appear mid- to late
summer. 23–30cm/9–12in. Excellent for sun or shade on any
well-drained soil, especially light sandy types. Trim back
annually mid-spring. Planting distance: 38–45cm/15–18in.

■ Five groundcover plants for covering a large area quickly

These are extremely vigorous and need plenty of space or
cutting back and dividing to keep them within bounds.

• **Larger periwinkle** (*Vinca major*) Shrubby carpeting or trailing plant with good shade tolerance. Provides excellent evergreen cover, except on poorly drained soils or in very dry
exposed habitats. Blue or white star-shaped flowers in spring.
Planting distance: 45cm/18in.

• **Lyme grass** (*Elymus arenarius*) Beautiful grass with fantasti-
cally rapid spread by means of underground runners. Excellent
for stabilizing loose soil. Broad blue-grey leaves, about
60cm/2ft long. Best in full sun; any well-drained soil. Planting
distance: 45–60cm/1½–2ft.

• *Pachysandra terminalis* Evergreen shrubby plant,
8–10cm/3–4in high, that provides excellent groundcover in
dry shade on acid or alkaline soils. Spreads by underground
stolons to form carpet of short densely leaved stems. Spikes of
small white flowers in spring. Planting distance: 30cm/12in.

• **Persian ivy** (*Hedera colchica*) An ivy that grows well in both
sun and deep shade. 15–23cm/6–9in high. Large, thick, dark
green leaves. 'Dentata Variegata' has creamy yellow leaf mar-
gins. Planting distance: 90–120cm/3–4ft.

• *Symphoricarpos* x *chenaultii* 'Hancock' Deciduous suckering shrub, 60cm/2ft high, providing fairly dense cover in sun
or moderate shade. Suitable for all well-drained soils. Small
pink or purple berries are produced on the arching or prostrate branches. Planting distance: 90cm/3ft.

■ Five groundcover plants for the shrub border

Planted in bold drifts, these low-growing plants contrast
particularly well with large shrubs.

• **Christmas box** (*Sarcococca humilis*) Low suckering shrub
effective in moister humus-rich soils; will tolerate drier sites if
shaded. Glossy evergreen leaves; small highly fragrant white
flowers in winter. 23–38cm/9–15in. Planting distance:
30cm/12in.

• **Creeping dogwood** (*Cornus canadensis*) Herbaceous perennial that requires an acid, fairly moist soil and partial shade.

Creeping roots. Reaches 10–15cm/4–6in in height. In early summer dense heads of tiny yellow-green flowers appear, each surrounded by four white bracts. These are followed by red berries. Planting distance: 30cm/12in.

• **Elephant's ears** (*Bergenia* species/hybrids) Evergreen perennials with large, often glossy, dark green leaves. Some develop purple tints in winter. Clusters of bell-shaped flowers appear in spring: shades of pink, red or white. Tolerates sun or shade, any soil. Planting distance: 23–60cm/9–24in.

• **Ling** (*Calluna vulgaris*) Hummock-forming heather that provides good dense evergreen cover in sunny sites on acid soils. Height 15–45cm/6–18in. Many varieties,with flowers in white, pink and purple, and often with attractively coloured (eg gold or red) foliage. Erect flower spikes borne in late summer. Trim off dead flowers. Planting distance: 23–45cm/9–18in.

• **Winter-flowering heather** (*Erica carnea*, also known as *E. herbacea*) Popular heathers, forming dense mats of evergreen foliage, covered in winter with pink, red or white flowers. Good varieties are 'Springwood Pink' and 'Springwood White'. Grows in an open sunny position; one of the few heathers that tolerate chalky soil. Trim off dead flowers in spring. Planting distance: 30–38cm/12–15in.

■ **Five groundcover plants for rose beds**

There is no need to have bare soil under rose bushes: the following plants provide an appealing alternative. If you feel that complete cover may hamper feeding, pruning and other activities, a compromise is to use low-growing plants just to edge the beds.

• **Catmint** (*Nepeta x faassenii*) Herbaceous perennial with small grey-green leaves that are pungently aromatic. Small lavender-blue flowers in summer. Height 23cm/9in. Needs full sun and a well-drained soil. Trim back annually in spring. Ideal for edging a bed. Planting distance: 30cm/12in.

• **Creeping Jenny** (*Lysimachia nummularia*) Attractive perennial groundcover for moist soils, sun or partial shade. Its numerous trailing stems root at joints. Small closely spaced leaves, buttercup-like yellow flowers in summer. 2.5–5cm/1–2in. Planting distance: 30cm/12in.

• **London pride** (*Saxifraga umbrosa*) Useful evergreen perennial either for edging or carpeting. Sprays of pale pink flowers in spring. Height 30cm/12in when in flower. Planting distance: 30cm/12in.

• **Self-heal** (*Prunella grandiflora*) Perennial with small evergreen leaves and prostrate stems that take root freely. In summer short erect stems carry spikes of tubular rose-purple flowers. 'Loveliness' has pink flowers. Likes moist soil and sun or shade. Planting distance: 30cm/12in.

• **Shrubby veronica** (*Hebe pinguifolia* 'Pagei') Evergreen shrub, 15–22cm/6–9in high, whose small blue-grey leaves provide dense cover. Small spikes of white flowers in summer. Needs full sun and well-drained soil. Ideal as an edger. Planting distance: 38cm/15in.

VEGETABLES

Vegetables grown at home and used immediately after gathering have a much better flavour than those bought in the shops. Contrary to popular belief, it is not necessary to have a large garden. Various small vegetables do well in containers on a patio, or in patches in a flowerbed or border. There are several vegetables, too, for the greenhouse, and even for growing in partial shade. It is possible to have an all-round supply: many people especially appreciate fresh produce in the depths of winter.

As an alternative to the traditional method of arranging vegetables in rows, the "deep-bed" system allows you to grow more crops in the space available, because the plants are closer together. The crops are grown in blocks or bands across the 1.2m/4ft wide beds, which are separated by 30–45cm/12–18in wide paths, from which you work at all times, except when digging. Initially you should prepare the beds by double-digging (see p36) and adding plenty of manure or garden compost. Repeat the double-digging every 3–4 years: in the intervening years, use normal single digging. Rotate crops to get the best from the soil.

■ Five vegetables for growing bags

The best containers for vegetables are proprietary growing bags, used once only for long-term crops such as tomatoes, or several times for quick-maturing kinds such as radishes. Alternatives are large troughs or tubs filled with a good loam-based potting compost – for example, John Innes No. 2 or an equivalent soilless type. Keep well-watered in dry weather.

• **Carrots** Round or stump-rooted varieties are best for containers. They can be sown early spring–early summer. Thin out to 5cm/2in apart each way when large enough to handle.

• **Dwarf French beans** Tender bushy plants which should not be sown until late spring. Modern varieties with stringless pods are best. Space seeds 30cm/12in apart each way. Once cropping starts, pick pods regularly before they become too large.

• **Onion, spring or salad** Grown for their slightly swollen stems, which are usually chopped for salads. The onion flavour

is light – powerful but not overpowering as in normal onions.
Sow early–late spring. No thinning needed – simply pull the
onions when large enough for use.

• **Radishes** Popular, easily grown salad vegetables. They
mature in a matter of weeks, so make successional sowings
from early spring to early autumn. Thin out seedlings to
2.5cm/1in apart each way. Keep well watered: radishes like
plenty of moisture.

• **Tomatoes** For containers use the dwarf outdoor bush types,
which grow to only 30cm/12in. Sow early spring in a heated
greenhouse; plant out late spring when danger of frost is over.
Space 45cm/18in apart each way. Feed well with proprietary
tomato fertilizer. Need a warm sunny spot.

■ Four compact popular vegetables

These small-growing varieties are especially recommended
if you have limited space.

• **Broad bean 'The Sutton'** Dwarf compact variety for sowing
between early spring and mid-summer, from late autumn to
late winter under cloches. Likes fertile well-drained soil in sun.
Sow seeds 23cm/9in apart each way.

• **Brussels sprout 'Peer Gynt'** Dwarf compact variety with
large crops of closely packed medium-size sprouts mid-late
autumn. Sow in succession from early to mid-spring. Plant
75cm/2½ft apart each way. Needs well-firmed fertile soil in
a sheltered sunny position.

• **Cabbage 'Hispi'** Popular cabbage with delicious small pointed heads. Quick grower. Make two or three sowings from mid-
spring to mid-summer for summer and autumn crops. Space
30–35cm/12–14in apart each way.

• **Lettuce 'Tom Thumb'** Quick-maturing small lettuce for the
summer. Sow early to mid-spring. Thin seedlings to 20cm/8in
apart each way. Grow in an open position with well-drained
fairly rich soil containing plenty of humus. Likes plenty of
moisture, so water daily in dry periods.

■ Four highly productive vegetables

Some vegetables give much bigger returns than others from
the available space.

• **Climbing French beans** These produce many more pods
than the dwarf French beans. Sow late spring to mid-summer
for summer and autumn crops. Well-drained fertile soil in full
sun. Sow seeds 8–10cm/3–4in apart in a row. Provide each
plant with a 1.8m/6ft bamboo cane.

• **Courgettes** Small marrows with 15cm/6in long fruits in
abundance during summer and autumn – provided that you

pick them regularly. There are green- and yellow-fruited varieties. A warm sunny spot, well-drained soil. Sow courgettes mid-spring in a greenhouse and plant out in the early summer, 90cm/3ft apart each way.

• **Peas, edible-podded** Far more productive than "ordinary" peas: you cook and eat the entire pods while still young and tender. A good variety is 'Sugar Snap'. Sow mid-spring to early summer. Scatter seeds about 5–8cm/2–3in apart in a 15cm/6in wide furrow. Support with tall twiggy sticks (height is 1.5–1.8m/5–6ft). Open sunny spot and moist fertile soil give best results.

• **Runner beans** Tender climbers producing huge crops of pods in summer and into autumn, if grown in a sheltered sunny position and rich moist soil. Like lots of water in summer. Sow late spring, 15cm/6in apart. Grow up 1.8m/6ft tall supports, such as canes (formed into a wigwam), bean poles or bean netting.

■ Five vegetables for winter/spring crops

The vegetable plot can be just as productive in winter or spring as in summer, especially if you grow the following staple crops for winter use.

• **Kale 'Thousand Headed'** Very hardy cabbage, producing an abundance of delicious leaves and shoots. Sow mid- to late spring, setting plants 45cm/18in apart each way. Best grown in fertile soil, but tolerates poor soils.

• **Leeks** Very hardy, long growing season. Leeks like fertile well-drained soil. Sow outdoors early to mid-spring, transplant in late spring or early summer. Plant 15cm/6in apart, in rows 30cm/12in apart. Drop each plant into 15cm/6in deep dibber hole; water well.

• **Parsnips** A root vegetable with a long growing season. Sow late winter or early spring. Small varieties (generally preferred) should be spaced 8cm/3in apart in rows 20cm/8in apart. Needs deep well-drained soil, which must not have been manured for at least a year before sowing. Tolerates lightly shaded spot.

• **Sprouting broccoli** Purple and white, with small leafy flowerheads on short stalks. The young succulent "spears" are pleasantly flavoured. Hardy: extremely useful for cold areas and poor soils. Mature mid-winter to late spring. They are large plants and need a long growing season, so are not suitable for very limited space. Sow mid- or late spring and set plants out at 67cm/27in apart each way.

• **Swedes** Grown for their swollen roots, which have a sweet taste. Best in a light well-drained firm soil, not recently

manured. Sow mid-spring to early summer, in rows 38cm/
15in apart. Thin seedlings to 23cm/9in apart.

■ Five vegetables for the greenhouse

The cool or unheated greenhouse can produce vegetables in
summer and through to autumn, and salad crops in winter. All are suitable for growing bags.

• **Cucumber** Best to grow the all-female varieties. Crop during
summer and autumn. Need humid atmosphere and minimum
night temperature of 16°C/60°F. Sow seeds mid-spring, one
per pot, and germinate at 24°C/75°F. Plant two per growing
bag and provide supports for the stems, such as horizontal
wires fixed to one wall.

• **Egg plant (aubergine)** Grown for egg-shaped fruits, sum-
mer/autumn. Minimum night temperature 13°C/55°F. Dryish
air, some sunshine. Sow seeds early spring; germinate at
18°C/65°F. Plant when 15cm/6in high, three per growing bag.
Feed well with tomato fertilizer.

• **Lettuce (winter)** Winter lettuce can be grown in a cool or
unheated greenhouse. Try 'Marmer' for cool, 'May Queen' for
unheated. Sow mid-autumn (germination temperature
10–16°C/50–60°F) and plant 20cm/8in apart each way. Needs
maximum light, a dry atmosphere and plenty of fresh air.

• **Sweet peppers (capsicum)** Grown for fruits,
summer/autumn. Minimum night temperature 13°C/55°F.
Dryish air, some sunshine. Sow seeds early spring; germinate
at 18°C/65°F. Plant when 15cm/6in high, three per growing
bag. Feed well with tomato fertilizer.

• **Tomatoes** Most popular summer/autumn greenhouse vegetable. Conditions and cultivation as for sweet peppers. Use
growing bag crop supports. Rub out sideshoots. Pinch out
growing point when 4–5 trusses of fruits produced. Feed well
with tomato fertilizer.

■ Three vegetables for growing in shade

Most vegetables need an open sunny site, but the following can be grown in shade, provided that it's not too
heavy, nor shady for the entire day.

• **Leaf beet (similar to seakale beet)** Grown for its leaves,
which are used like spinach, and for the thick white leaf-stalks
which can be cooked separately as a delicately flavoured vegetable. Sow mid-spring for summer crops. Thin seedlings to
15cm/6in apart each way. Water heavily in dry weather.

• **Lettuce (summer)** Likes a moist humus-rich soil. Sow seeds
mid-spring to late summer. Thin to 30cm/12in apart each way
(23cm/9in for dwarf varieties). Water well in dry weather.

• **Spinach (summer)** Likes soil rich in organic matter. Fast grower: needs plenty of water in summer. Sow seeds in succession from early to late spring in rows 30cm/12in apart. Thin to 15cm/6in apart.

■ Four vegetables for growing in flower borders

Some vegetables are ornamental, and will not look at all incongruous in a flower border.

• **Beetroot** Purplish leaves and stems look attractive in bold patches at the front of the border. Globe or round-rooted varieties are recommended and are harvested in summer. Sow seeds mid-spring. Thin to 10cm/4in apart each way.

• **Lettuce** Variety 'Salad Bowl', with deeply cut and frilled leaves, makes a good edging to a border or bed. Pick individual leaves as and when required throughout summer and into autumn. See summer lettuce (opposite); thin seedlings to 30cm/12in apart each way.

• **Rhubarb chard** A variety of leaf beet (see above) but with red stalks. Highly colourful in a bold group.

• **Sweet corn** Grown for its cobs which mature in summer or autumn. Broad grassy foliage attractive in a bold group in the middle or at the back of a border – the plants are tall. Likes plenty of sun and well-drained soil. Raise in single pots under glass in mid-spring; plant out 30cm/12in apart each way in early summer.

■ Fourteen culinary herbs

Most herbs are easy to grow. The following selection provides a variety of flavours to complement home-grown vegetables and enhance everyday food. Site the herb patch in a sunny well-drained spot near the kitchen. Some of these herbs will also grow well in containers.

• **Angelica** (*Angelica archangelica*) Aromatic leaves have various uses; stems are candied and used in cake decoration. Biennial grown from seed. 180cm/6ft tall. Sown outdoors in late summer, under a cloche in cold areas. Transplant to 30cm/12in apart the following spring. Remove flower heads.

• **Basil** (*Ocimum basilicum*) The ideal culinary complement to tomatoes. Tender, liable to be killed by frost. Sow seed in heated greenhouse in early spring. Plant out 30cm/12in apart in early summer after hardening off. Remove flower stalks. Plants can be lifted, potted and taken indoors in early autumn for autumn or winter use. Pick leaves as required throughout summer. Pinch out flowers as they appear.

• **Borage** (*Borago officinalis*) Hardy annual whose leaves taste of cucumber; chopped young leaves and whole flowers can be added to salads or used to flavour cool summer punches. Grows to 90cm/3ft and bears blue flowers. Sow indoors in early spring and thin seedlings to 30cm/12in apart each way.

• **Chives** (*Allium schoenoprasum*) Hardy perennial of the onion family. Grown for its grassy leaves which are chopped and used in savoury dishes, soups and salads. Initially raise from seeds sown outdoors in early spring. Thin to 15cm/6in apart. Cut off flowers. Divide clumps every 2–3 years; replant 15cm/6in apart. Ideal for containers. Cut leaves as required, just above soil.

• **Dill** (*Anethum graveolens*) Grown for aromatic leaves, used to flavour salads and fish dishes. Feathery green-blue foliage and heads of tiny yellow flowers. Sow seeds successively from mid-spring to early summer for continuous supply of young leaves. Thin seedlings to 30cm/12in apart. Pick fresh leaves as required when plants are 20cm/8in tall. Young leaves can also be dried for winter use.

• **Fennel** (*Foeniculum vulgare*) Attractive perennial, 180cm/6ft or more high, feathery blue-tinged foliage and yellow flowers. Grown for young shoots; also seeds, used in sweet and savoury dishes. Can be grown successfully in pots. Initially sow seeds in early spring outdoors. Thin seedlings to 30cm/12in apart. Established clumps can be divided every 3 or 4 years. Pick fresh leaves regularly throughout summer. In autumn collect fully ripe dry seeds.

• **French tarragon** (*Artemisia dracunculus*) Shrub, 90cm/3ft tall, spreading by underground runners. Buy young plants and plant in late spring, 60cm/2ft apart each way. Lift and replant a few vigorous runners every 3 or 4 years. Discard older portions of plant. Suitable for large containers. Cut young leaves as needed in summer. Leaves for drying can be cut in early or mid-summer. Protect with straw or bracken in winter.

• **Marjoram** Cooks use the young leaves. Suitable for containers. SWEET MARJORAM (*Origanum majorana*) is a half-hardy annual. Seeds can be sown outdoors each year in late spring; thin seedlings to 30cm/12in apart each way. Leaves may be dried for winter use. POT MARJORAM (*Origanum onites*) is a hardy dwarf shrub, best propagated from heel cuttings in early summer. Cut plants hard back in late winter.

• **Mint** A hardy perennial. The common mint is SPEARMINT (*Mentha spicata*). APPLEMINT (*Mentha* x *villosa alopecuroides*), also popular, has a more subtle flavour. Mint does best in moist soil and is ideal for a container (or sunken bucket) which will control its vigorous growth. Lift and divide the roots in early spring each year. Pick fresh young leaves as required throughout summer and into autumn. Leaves can also be dried for winter use and to make mint tea.

• **Parsley** (*Petroselinum crispum*) Biennial best grown as an annual. Overwinters successfully under cloches. There are several varieties, some with flat leaves, but curly-leaved varieties are most often grown. Prefers moist soil and semi-shade. Sow seeds outdoors in early spring and thin seedlings to 10cm/4in apart. Seeds can take up to 8 weeks to germinate. Ideal for growing in pots. Pick fresh as required.

• **Rosemary** (*Rosmarinus officinalis*) Blue-flowered shrub with grey-green needle-shaped aromatic leaves. Buy and plant a young bush in spring. Propagate from heel cuttings rooted in sandy compost in early summer. Prune in spring to encourage a compact bushy habit. Makes a good pot plant – keep indoors during coldest part of winter. Pick fresh leaves as required. Pick leaves for drying in summer.

• **Sage** (*Salvia officinalis*) Small evergreen shrub, 45–60cm/1½–2ft high, ideal for containers. Sow seed under glass in early spring. Plant out young plants in late spring, 30cm/12in apart each way. Propagate from heel cuttings in summer. Renew shrubs every 3–4 years. Pick leaves as required; or cut for drying in the active growing season.

• **Sweet bay** (*Laurus nobilis*) Attractive evergreen tree grown for aromatic leaves. Ideal for a pot or tub. Grow in a sheltered spot. Buy and plant a young bush in spring. Propagate from semi-ripe cuttings in late summer. Clip tree to shape if desired – for example, a formal pyramid. Place pot-grown trees in frost-free greenhouse during the winter. Pick young leaves as required and dry them slowly in the dark.

• **Thyme** (*Thymus vulgaris*) Small perennial bush, about 25cm/10in high. Beautiful scent. Seeds sown outdoors in early spring germinate fairly readily; seedlings should be thinned to 30cm/12in apart. Trim plants after flowering to encourage compact growth. Renew every 3–4 years. Propagate by division or heel cuttings. Ideal for containers. Whether for drying or immediate use, pick leaves before flowering.

FRUITS

Given a sunny spot and fertile, well-drained soil, most fruits are easy to grow. The greatest problem is damage from birds, which can wreak havoc on ripening crops unless you provide protection. Certain fruits, such as plums, cherries and bush fruits, need defending during the winter, as birds, especially bullfinches will attack and devour overwintering buds.

Bird repellents have a low success rate. Small fruit trees and bushes are better protected by draping them with lightweight nylon or plastic netting. Strawberries should be covered with netting on 45cm/18in high posts. You can safeguard individual

fruits by securing paper, muslin or perforated polythene bags or sleeving around them, provided that the tree or crop is not too large. Cardboard collars around the stalks of tree fruits will prevent birds from perching close enough to peck the fruit – again, only feasible on a small scale.

There are various ways to grow fruits even where space is restricted. For example, you can grow dwarf trees in tubs on a patio; or you can train trees flat, alongside a garden path or against a wall or fence. Several kinds of fruits can be grown on single stems to reduce space consumption (see p59). Even raspberries do not have to be grown in long space-consuming rows. Instead, you can tie each plant to a single upright post driven into the ground. After fruiting, cut down to ground level the old canes which have fruited, and tie in the young ones for next year.

■ Six fruits for patio containers

Y ou can grow tree fruits either as dwarf bush trees or as dwarf pyramids grafted (by the nurseryman) onto special dwarfing rootstocks. Apples and pears are available as "family" trees – several varieties on one tree. Start off trees in 30–45cm/ 12–18in diameter clay pots, eventually moving them onto 45– 60cm/1½–2ft diameter tubs. Use a loam-based potting compost such as John Innes No. 3. For pruning techniques refer to a specialist fruit book. See also pp58/9.

• **Apples** Grow as dwarf bush or dwarf pyramid. Choose a "family" tree on a dwarfing rootstock (M9 or M27).

• **Cherries** Grow as bush tree or dwarf pyramid. Choose the self-fertile variety 'Stella' and make sure it's on the dwarfing rootstock called 'Colt'.

• **Peaches** Grow as bush tree. 'Duke of York' and 'Hale's Early' are good varieties. Pollinate flowers by hand, dabbing the centre of each in turn with a soft artist's brush.

• **Pears** Grow as dwarf bush or dwarf pyramid. Choose a "family" tree containing several varieties. Trees should be on dwarfing rootstocks.

• **Plums** Good variety is 'Victoria', grown as dwarf bush or dwarf pyramid. Unlike so many other plums, this is self-fertile. The tree should be on the dwarf rootstock 'Pixy'.

• **Strawberries** Seldom do well in a strawberry barrel – a full-sized wooden barrel, in the sides of which are small holes. Plant them instead in 25cm/10in clay flowerpots of loam-based potting compost such as John Innes No. 2. Three plants will fit in each pot. Alternatively, grow in proprietary Tower-pots. Good varieties are 'Tenira' and 'Pantagruella'.

■ Two fruits for walls

The following popular soft fruits can be trained flat against a wall or fence in any part of the garden. Also suitable for this treatment are espalier trained apples and pears, and fan-trained peaches, plums and cherries. (The various fruit tree forms are discussed on pp59–60.)

• **Blackberries** Cultivated blackberries like 'Bedford Giant', 'Himalaya Giant', 'Oregon Thornless' and 'Smoothstem' carry heavy crops of large fruits in summer/autumn. Normally only one plant is needed for an average family. Tolerates partial shade. Train the long stems to a fan shape, on a system of horizontal wires. After fruiting, cut out the old fruited stems completely and replace them by young ones which will fruit the following year.

• **Hybrid berries** These are crosses between such fruits as the blackberry, raspberry and dewberry. Most hybrid berries are not as vigorous as the blackberry and are therefore more suited to the small garden. Well-known hybrid berries include 'John Innes', the loganberry (LY59 which is thorny, and L654 which is thornless), and the tayberry (ideal for very limited space). All these examples are grown in the same way as blackberries.

LAWNS

MAKING A LAWN

Most lawns are all too predictably square or rectangular, but you can often make a major aesthetic improvement by introducing curves. This also has the advantage of allowing you greater freedom to emphasize attractive garden features such as ornaments, pools or groupings of plants.

The proposed lawn site should be in full sun or receive sunlight for at least part of the day. Do not expect a lawn to grow in a heavily shaded site (for example, under the dense canopy of a large tree) nor in excessively wet conditions. Consider laying drains if the natural drainage is poor.

A lawn will only be as good as its preparation. Faults in new lawns are usually caused by factors such as inadequate soil preparation, sowing unevenly, using poor-quality seed, or incorrect laying of turves. All these can result in weak, sparse growth that will be susceptible to pests and diseases, and allow mosses and weeds to take root. Advice on controlling the most common troubles that affect lawns is given on pp148–9): apply control measures as soon as you see any symptoms.

■ Seven essential steps to preparing the site

Begin at least 2–3 months before the projected dates for sowing or turfing. This gives time for the soil to settle and for weeds to be brought under control.

• **Clearing the site** If you have a new site, clear away all builders' rubble and remove any heaps of subsoil: do not spread subsoil over the topsoil. Dig out tree stumps. Eradicate all perennial weeds by spraying, during the growing season, with a weedkiller containing glyphosate. If there is less than 15cm/6in of topsoil on site, buy some and spread it when the weeds are dead.

• **Levelling** If you want a really level lawn, proceed as follows. Hammer in a wooden master peg at a selected point, leaving 10cm/4in above the surface. Now, drive in more pegs at 180cm/6ft intervals to form a grid system. Establish the master peg at the required level then, working from it, adjust the other pegs with a straight-edged board and spirit level until they align with the master peg. Next, add or remove soil (subsoil or topsoil) until the soil surface is level either with the top of each peg or comes up to a predetermined peg marking.

• **Digging** A lawn site should be dug deeply – by double digging if exceptionally compacted, otherwise by single digging (see p35). When digging heavy soils, incorporate gritty

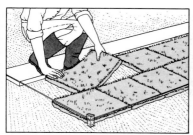

Laying turves

Correcting the level

Rolling

Filling gaps

Edging

material to improve soil texture and porosity. Also, add well-rotted farmyard manure or garden compost. On sandy soils incorporate either of these materials to improve moisture retention and encourage deeper rooting.

• **Draining** If the site is prone to waterlogging, you may need to install a drainage system to get rid of excess water. See p36.

• **Soil pH** If the soil is very acid (low pH) or very alkaline (high pH) the grass may not grow well. The ideal pH for lawns is between 6 and 6.5 (slightly acid). Simple test kits are available for measuring soil pH. If the soil is too acid, apply ground chalk or ground limestone. If unsure how much is needed, apply 70–135g per sq metre/2–4oz per sq yard. On alkaline soils reduce pH by adding acidic peat.

• **Final preparations** Several weeks before sowing or turfing, you must create a firm, even, fine-particled, soil surface. First, break down clods and lumps using a garden fork or metal rake (or rotary cultivator if the site is large). Next, firm or consolidate the soil – on small sites by treading systematically with the weight on your heels, on large sites by using a garden roller. Do not break down and firm when the soil is wet. Next, rake level, remove stones and debris, and firm again. Then give a final light raking.

• **Fertilizer application** 7 to 10 days before sowing, apply a proprietary pre-sowing fertilizer according to maker's instructions. Thoroughly rake this into the surface.

■ Two types of turf

When buying turf, always go to a specialist supplier: then you will have a choice of proper lawn grasses (see pp131–2), and the turf will be (or should be!) free from weeds and cut to a uniform depth.

• **Field-grown turf** This is the most popular. Usually sold in 90cm/3ft by 30cm/1ft pieces, each rolled up for delivery. The pieces will be of uniform thickness.

• **Seedling turf** This comes in large lightweight rolls and is well-rooted and of uniform thickness. It's raised on special nurseries. You can order exactly the kind of grass you want for particular uses, soil conditions or aspects (eg for chalky soil, shady conditions, etc).

■ Eight essential steps to laying turf

Turf is quick and quite easy to lay, although some people may find field-grown turf, with its layer of soil, somewhat heavy to handle. Field-grown turf is best laid in autumn, winter or early spring, when there is little or no risk of the ground drying out. Seedling turf should not be laid in winter, when cold weather prevents rapid establishment. Never lay turf in summer, when there is risk of drought, unless you can guarantee regular watering.

• **Storing turves** Ideally you should lay turves immediately they are delivered, although no harm will come to them if they are left rolled for a couple of days. If you have to delay laying any longer, unroll the turves and lay them on a spare piece of soil – do not leave them for more than a week, though, or they will start to root.

• **Where to start** Start laying turves on one side of the site, by putting down one row of field-grown turves, or a roll of seedling turf. Ensure each piece of turf is laid as close as possible to the previous one. Do not at any time stand on the prepared bed, but work forward, facing the bare soil, standing or kneeling on broad planks laid on the turf.

• **Laying the rest** Stagger successive lines of field-grown turf by using half turves in alternate rows (just like laying bricks in a wall). The turves will then bond together quickly and well. Rolls of seedling turf are simply laid in strips: follow suppliers' instructions.

• **Minor adjustments** Keep a constant watch on the soil level and have a bucket of ordinary soil and a garden rake handy for adjusting minor irregularities. Never attempt to level a piece of turf by beating it down: instead remove a little soil.

• **Firming the turf** When laying is complete, firm the turf by rolling with a light garden roller to eliminate air pockets and help settling.

• **Filling gaps** Fill any gaps in the joints with ordinary fine soil, brushing it well in with a stiff brush. Trim the lawn's edges with a half-moon iron.

• **Watering** Water the new lawn thoroughly and regularly in dry periods especially if turf is laid in spring or summer when the soil is particularly susceptible to drying out, or it will shrink and may fail to root.

• **Mowing** When the grass begins to grow, cut it lightly with the mower. With seedling turf, give an initial cut after 2 or 3 weeks and do not cut closer than 2.5cm/1in during the first 6 weeks after laying. Thereafter, mow as for established lawns.

■ **Three grass-seed mixtures for different purposes**

A new lawn created from seed is cheaper than turf but takes longer to establish. Grass seed is supplied as a mixture of different kinds of grasses. Buy a proprietary mixture suited to the use to which you want to put the lawn, not forgetting soil conditions and aspect. If you have a problem site (for example, excessively dry, very thin chalky, or very acid heathland), seek advice from a specialist supplier.

• **For a fine ornamental lawn** If you want a lawn like green velvet, choose a seed mixture containing fine-leaved grasses, such as the bent grasses (*Agrostis*) and fescues (*Festuca*). Such lawns need a lot of attention to keep them looking good, including regular frequent mowing. Do not subject to heavy use. (Not suitable for children's play areas.)

• **For a hardwearing utility lawn** For a well-used lawn, you need tough hardwearing grasses, with broader leaves than the fescues and bents and therefore a coarser texture. Seed mixtures contain perennial rye grass (*Lolium perenne*) and meadow grasses (*Poa*). These lawns need less frequent mowing than a fine ornamental lawn.

• **For shade** Special mixtures available for lightly shaded sites include, for example, rough-stalked meadow grass (*Poa trivialis*) or fine-leaved fescue (*Festuca tenuifolia*).

■ Nine stages in creating a lawn from seed

The two most suitable periods for sowing grass seeds are early autumn and spring, when the soil is warm and moisture usually plentiful. Together, these conditions encourage a quick germination period – about 10 days. If weeds appear with the grass seedlings, don't worry: they will help to "nurse" the grass, and as soon as mowing begins most of them will die out and disappear.

• **Judging the conditions** Always sow during a period of calm dry weather when the surface of the seedbed is dry and soil will not adhere to your boots. There should, however, be moisture just below the surface.

• **Calculating the amount of seed** Grass seed is sown at the rate of 35–70g per sq metre/1–2oz per sq yard. Aim for the midway point – 50g per sq metre/1½oz per sq yard.

• **Creating the furrows** These must be shallow. Make them by lightly raking the site in one direction just before sowing.

• **Sowing** BY HAND: best for small areas. First, divide the seed into two equal portions. Sow half the seeds by traversing the plot lengthways, then sow the remaining half crossways. This method gives a more even coverage than a single application. For precision sowing, mark off the plot with strings into square metres or square yards. BY SEED DRILL: for larger areas. If you don't own a drill, it may be worth hiring one. Ensure that it can be calibrated to apply grass seeds at the required rate. To check that a drill is applying the correct quantity, mark out two separate square metre (or square yard) areas on a strip of concrete, hessian or the like. Scatter the desired quantity of seeds by hand on one square, then run the drill over the other square. The density of seeds should be equal in the two squares. Apply the seeds to the seedbed in parallel strips, using the previous run's wheeltrack as a guide. As with handsowing, sow half the seed lengthways, and half crossways.

• **Covering the seeds** After sowing, lightly rake over the seedbed, filling in the shallow furrows so that the seeds are covered over. Do this with care: if the seeds are buried too deeply they may not germinate, and if you disturb the soil too much the seed distribution may be uneven.

• **Watering** If after a few days there has been no rainfall, water gently but thoroughly with a garden sprinkler. Do not use a hose: the jet may redistribute the seeds, and also create a surface crust which may inhibit germination.

• **Protection against birds** Grass seeds are often treated with bird repellents to prevent them from being eaten. But a more serious problem created by birds is that of dust-bathing. Prevent this by stretching black thread 8–10cm/3–4in taut above the seedbed, or by laying some leafless twiggy brushwood lightly over the bed.

• **Firming the soil** The soil surface is often lightly lifted at germination. Therefore, when the grass is 5–8cm/2–3in high, lightly roll when the surface is dry, using a light garden roller.

• **Mowing** A new lawn should be mown for the first time when the grass is about 8cm/3in high. The mower's blades should be really sharp, and set to remove only 2.5cm/1in of growth: that is, the height of cut should be 5cm/2in. Thereafter mow the lawn regularly, gradually reducing the height of cut to 2.5cm/1in. During the first year, do not cut closer than 1.25cm/½in.

■ Two alternatives to the closely mown lawn

To create a more natural look, at least in one area of the garden, it is well worth considering the following labour-saving alternatives.

• **Long-grass meadow** By letting the grass grow long, you can form a natural-looking "meadow". This may be ideal for a bank, although any flat area could also be treated like this. To make the meadow more interesting, put in some flowering plants – for example, spring-flowering bulbs, including miniature daffodils, crocuses and fritillaries. The grass will need cutting once or twice in the year, but don't cut until the bulbs' leaves have completely died down – early summer. You may need to cut again later in the summer. Use a scythe or a garden power trimmer, and rake up the "hay". Alternatively, you could create a wild flower meadow, planted with a mix of grass and native flowering plants suited to soil and locality. Sow a mixture of grass seeds and wild flower seeds from a specialist supplier. Cut annually with a scythe or power trimmer after the flowers have faded in early autumn.

• **Chamomile lawn** Chamomile (*Anthemis nobilis*), used for making lawns for centuries, is a low-growing evergreen perennial with creeping stems that root as they spread. The dark green finely divided leaves are aromatic when crushed underfoot: but don't walk on it too much. The best form for lawns is the non-flowering 'Treneague', which grows to 2.5–5cm/1–2in. Chamomile is tolerant of dry sunny sites and lighter soils, but dislikes any degree of shade. It tends to die out in patches and does not completely suppress weeds; hand-weed from time to time. To form the lawn, plant young plants, about 15cm/6in

Using a hollow-tine aerator

Using an aerating machine

apart each way, in spring. Carefully trim in late summer, using a mower or shears. Don't trim hard, as you would an ordinary lawn: just remove any over-long shoots.

CARING FOR A LAWN

Lawn care requires an annual programme of various operations. If all you do is mow, you will end up with a thin or patchy lawn that becomes invaded by weeds and moss. For a healthy carpet of green, you must feed, water, remove rubbish and dead material, relieve the lawn of compaction, and perform various other tasks. There are no short cuts. A large neglected lawn is an eyesore. If time for routine maintenance is limited, better to have only a small well-kept lawn and devote the rest of the garden to more labour-saving schemes, such as groundcover.

■ **Four ways to ensure healthy growth**

Carry out these important operations in early autumn, when the mowing season is over.

• **Scarifying** The vigorous use of a rake or special tool to remove dead material, known as thatch, from the lawn. The thatch lies between the soil surface and foliage. If it becomes too thick, it can impede moisture penetration. Water will reach the soil only after prolonged rain or artificial watering. Fertilizers may not penetrate. Dense thatch also prevents air from reaching the roots of the grass, and can lead to diseases, less drought resistance, and water lying on the surface. You can scarify with a spring-tine lawn rake, a special scarifying rake or with a motorized scarifier. Work methodically, first lengthways and then crossways.

• **Raking** The aim is to remove loose surface material and debris and to control creeping weeds. Use a spring-tine lawn rake, less vigorously than you would when scarifying. Rake in autumn to remove fallen leaves, which can smother the grass; also in early spring, before the first mowing of the year, to remove any debris left over from winter. After application of moss-killers (in autumn or early spring), rake fairly vigorously to remove dead moss.

• **Aerating** Spiking a lawn, or making slits in it. This relieves compaction caused by heavy use and by mowing, and thus allows air and water into the soil. Carry out light surface aeration in spring and summer, and deep aeration in early autumn. There are various tools one can use. Some merely prick the surface – useful only for breaking up light surface compaction. To tackle deeper compaction, choose a tool that gives 10–15cm/4–6in penetration. For small areas use a garden fork, inserting it vertically, and then easing it backwards and forwards fractionally. Space each set of holes 10–15cm/4–6in apart. If the soil is heavy or waterlogged a hollow-tine aerator will give better results. Each hollow tine removes a core of soil, expelling it on the lawn surface. Sweep up the cores afterwards, then top-dress (see below). On heavier soils you will only need to hollow-tine every 3rd or 4th year. For large lawns, buy or hire an aerating machine, powered or hand-propelled. These usually have interchangeable, solid, hollow or wedge-shaped tines (the latter make slits in the lawn).

• **Top-dressing** The application of a mixture of loam, sand and peat to even out irregularities in the lawn surface and to improve the surface soil. On difficult soils (sands, clays, chalks), annual dressings progressively form an upper layer of better-quality soil. Carry out early autumn after aerating – but only when the grass is dry. First, mow the lawn short. Make up a mix of loam, lime-free horticultural sand and granulated sphagnum moss peat or coco fibre. A useful formula is 3 parts loam, 6 parts sand and 1 part peat. You can modify as necessary – eg less sand for a sandy soil, more for a heavy clay soil. The mixture should be fairly dry to make spreading easier. Broadcast the mix with a shovel, then work well into the base of the grass using the back of a wooden garden rake or a home-made lute. An average dressing is 1.8kg per sq metre/4lb per sq yard; but on very uneven lawns increase this to 3kg/6–7lb. If you cannot work in all the top-dressing, remove the surplus: it must not be allowed to lie on the surface. It may take 2 or 3 seasons of top-dressing to achieve a smooth level surface. Do not try to achieve perfection with a single dressing – if the grass is completely covered it may die. Once you have a satisfactory surface, there is no need for annual top-dressing unless the soil is poor.

■ Six ways to control weeds

The weeds most troublesome in lawns are coarse weed grasses and low-growing perennials of creeping or rosette-type growth, such as clover (*Trifolium*), speedwell (*Veronica*), daisy (*Bellis perennis*), dandelion (*Taraxacum officinale*) and plantain (*Plantago*). Moss is also another common lawn weed.

• **Regular lawn care** Regular mowing, feeding, watering and other aspects of lawn care will keep the lawn densely leaved and healthy, making it difficult for weeds to establish themselves. When mowing, use a grass box, which minimizes the spread of weeds.

• **Hand-weeding** A daisy grubber (like a two-pronged garden hand fork) is useful for dealing with scattered weeds. Remove the roots as well as the top-growth.

• **Spot treatment** Spot treating with a lawn weedkiller in aerosol or solid-stick form is a simple and economical method of control if there are only a few isolated weeds present.

• **Treating the whole lawn** If there are lots of weeds, treat the whole lawn with a selective lawn weedkiller, ideally one containing several active ingredients to control a wide range of weeds – eg mecoprop, MCPA or 2,4-D. Repeat treatment may be needed after 4–5 weeks. Most lawn weedkillers are sold in concentrated liquid form for dilution with water. Apply in spring or early autumn, ideally during fine warm conditions when the soil is thoroughly moist and grass growth is vigorous. For large areas use a pressure sprayer; for small areas use a watering can fitted with a dribble bar. Some lawn fertilizers incorporate weedkillers in dry form.

• **Weed grasses** These are not affected by selective lawn weedkillers. Instead use a knife to slash through leaves and roots. Do this repeatedly until eradicated. Large areas are best dug out, the hole filled in and the area re-seeded.

• **Moss control** Moss colonizes where poor fertility, lack of aeration, bad drainage, excessive shade or mowing too closely has resulted in weak sparse grass. Rectify these faults and kill the moss with a proprietary mosskiller applied in spring or early autumn, as directed by the maker. Mosskillers have to be diluted with water. Apply with a sprayer, or with a watering can fitted with a dribble bar. When the moss is dead (it turns black) rake it out with a lawn rake or other scarifying tool.

■ Five aspects of watering

Even in areas that apparently house a good rainfall, lawns can suffer from water shortage. In spring, summer or early autumn the grass can turn brown. Although it will usually recover, a period of temporary weakness encourages weeds. Watering is therefore essential in dry spells.

• **When to start** As soon as the first symptoms of drought appear – loss of resilience in the lawn and its colour becoming dull. The leaves then turn yellow, then brown. In spring or summer look out for these signs after there has been dry weather for 7–10 days, ignoring occasional light showers. Most grass roots are in the top 25–30cm/10–12in of soil. The first signs of drought are usually seen once the top 10–13cm/4–5in have dried out.

• **Frequency** Varies according to soil type. Clay soil holds more water than a loam soil, which holds more than a light sandy soil. Thus, the lighter the soil, the more frequently watering is needed. As a general guide, in dry sunny weather during the spring and summer a healthy well-maintained lawn on an average loam soil needs a thorough watering about once every 7 days.

• **Helping water to penetrate** If the soil is too dry for water to seep through, spike it shallowly beforehand.

• **How much** Frequent light watering is bad for a lawn. It encourages shallow rooting and the development of moss. Frequent heavy watering can also be harmful, because it encourages moss and grass diseases. So apply about 18 litres/ 4 gallons of water per square metre/yard (about 2.5cm/1in) per week. Or, better still, apply 1.25cm/½in of water every 3 days. You can measure this by standing a jam jar under the sprinkler and watering until it holds this depth of water.

• **Application methods** A sprinkler is best, whatever the lawn's size. There are static types, as well as rotary and oscillating kinds. Perforated plastic tubes are useful for grass paths and awkward places but give a less even application than sprinklers and should not be used for lawns.

■ Five aspects of feeding

Feeding a lawn strengthens and thickens the grass, making it more resistant to drought, diseases, weeds, moss and hard wear. It also maintains good colour and texture. Of course, feeding increases the growth rate, so more frequent mowing is called for.

• **Choosing fertilizer** Best to use a proprietary lawn fertilizer, which contains optimum amounts of the major foods: nitrogen which promotes lush green grass; phosphorus which aids root development; and potassium which hardens growth and increases resistance to disease, cold and drought. Use a granular lawn fertilizer for all major feeding. If a quick boost is needed in summer, use a liquid type.

• **Spring feeding** Spring is one of the two major feeding periods. Use a lawn fertilizer formulated for spring and summer use. It will be high in nitrogen, so that the grass will green quickly after the ravages of winter.

• **Summer feeding** After a good spring feed, it should not be necessary to feed in summer. But if the lawn looks "tired" you could give it a liquid feed, provided that the soil is thoroughly moist and the lawn is not suffering from drought.

• **Autumn feeding** Autumn is the second major feeding period. The fertilizer hardens the grass so that it overwinters well and gets off to a good start the following year. Use a lawn fertilizer specially formulated for autumn application – low in nitrogen, high in potash. Apply early autumn during mild settled weather.

• **Applying fertilizer** The amount to apply will be stated on the bag. Too much may damage or scorch the grass. Always apply when the grass is dry but the soil moist, preferably during cool showery weather. If rain does not fall within 48 hours you should water in the fertilizer. Do not feed during periods of drought. It is essential to put on fertilizers evenly and at the correct rate, so use a simple fertilizer distributor: several lawn-fertilizer manufacturers offer these. Calibrate the machine and test carefully by running over a newspaper or a concrete path to ensure that you have the correct rate of output. Then apply to the lawn in parallel strips using the previous run's wheel-tracks as a guide for each strip to prevent overlapping. Apply fertilizer in two batches at half the rate each time, going first lengthways and then crossways.

■ Six points to consider when mowing

Mowing too close (a common mistake) weakens the grass and allows moss and lawn weeds to become established. On the other hand, where lawns are allowed to grow too long, coarser grasses become increasingly dominant and finer grasses deteriorate. For best results you should mow regularly but not too closely. For guidance on choosing a mower see p31.

• **How often** Mow fine lawns at intervals of 2–3 days. Mow average lawns (that is, utility lawns containing rye grass) at least every 7 days and preferably every 3–5 days.

• **Height of cut** Varies according to the season and type of lawn. In spring and summer fine ornamental lawns should be cut to 0.75–1.25cm/¼–½in, while average utility lawns should be cut to 1.25–2.5/½–1in. Raise the height of cut in autumn and early spring (also in winter if the grass needs cutting then) to 2cm/¾in (fine lawns) or 2.5–5.75cm/1–1½in (average utility lawns).

• **Timing** It's best and easiest to mow when the grass is dry. Do not mow when the soil is very wet or the mower may churn up the grass.

• **Debris** Before mowing check the lawn to ensure there are no stones, twigs or other debris which may foul the mower. Wormcasts should be scattered with a stiff broom or besom – if the mower runs over casts it will flatten them, resulting in muddy patches which not only look unsightly but smother the grasses and prevent growth.

• **How to mow** If you want a neat striped effect (only obtainable with a mower that has a roller attachment), first mow across each end, plus any awkward places. Then mow the main part, in a systematic up and down sequence. It's best to vary the direction of mowing for each session. This helps smooth out irregularities in the mowing and control weed grasses. With wheeled rotary mowers and hover mowers direction of cut is not so important. However, you should still work to a methodical pattern, if only to save time and effort!

• **Clippings** If the mower is fitted with a grass-box – use it! If clippings are left on the lawn after each mowing they will lead to thatch, an increase in the worm population, and a greater incidence of diseases and weeds. On the other hand, clippings left in moderation will return foods to the soil and help to conserve moisture during dry weather.

■ Four mowing faults

The following symptoms mostly indicate a flawed mowing technique, or a mower that is damaged, incorrectly set or otherwise unsatisfactory.

• **Ribbing** A series of narrow parallel strips of alternating longer and shorter grass. Occurs with cylinder mowers that have a low cylinder speed and a small number of blades. Also occurs when the grass is too long for the mower setting – in which case increase the height of cut.

• **Corrugations** Irregular waves of corrugations left after mowing are caused by the grass always being mown in the same direction. Usually occur with powered mowers. Change the mowing pattern and vary the direction with successive cuts.

• **Lacerated grass** This is caused either by having blunt or incorrectly set mower blades, or by a machine with a damaged bottom cutting plate. Check the mower carefully and adjust or repair it as necessary.

• **Scalping** Occurs where there are irregularities in the lawn surface. Try increasing the height of cut and top-dressing to improve the level of the lawn. Major irregularities must be corrected by lifting the turf and adding or removing soil as necessary to solve the problem.

■ Three aspects of caring for banks and long grass

Slopes and long-grass areas need feeding and watering just as much as ordinary lawns, but cutting requires a rather different approach.

• **Gentle bank: short grass** Provided that the bank does not exceed 30° you should be able to cut it with a lightweight electric cylinder mower. Always mow along the bank, not up and down the slope, as this can be dangerous.

• **Steep bank: long grass** Never attempt to use a mower in these conditions. Instead, cut with a scythe or sickle. Long grass generally needs cutting only once or twice a year. Rake up the "hay" afterwards. (You can soften the slope of a steep bank by the cut-and-fill method: see p20).

• **Other long-grass areas** Areas with bulbs should be cut only when the bulbs' foliage has died down. Areas with meadow flowers are cut only when the flowers have died down. Generally once or twice a year is sufficient. Long-grass areas on the flat can be cut with a powered wheeled rotary mower, a strimmer or a motorized scythe (which you may be able to hire). Always rake up the "hay".

GARDEN DOCTOR

PREVENTION AND CONTROL

Pests and diseases do not spread their ills even-handedly throughout the plant world. Some plants, such as conifers, hardy annuals and shrub roses, are troubled rarely or never; others, such as bush roses, fruits and vegetables, may be affected by more than their fair share. You should bear in mind that the vast majority of pests and diseases can be tolerated – provided that the plants are healthy and well-fed and never allowed to go short of water. Do not underestimate the value of predatory insects such as hoverflies and insect and grub-devouring birds. Treatments for specific problems are recommended on the following pages. You are extremely unlikely to have to resort to many of these measures in any one year. Some plants are prone to attacks from certain pests (for example broad beans are prey to blackfly), or to diseases (many roses are being attacked by black spot). Look out for these and carry out control measures as soon as symptoms appear, to prevent a big build-up.

■ Six ways to avoid pests and diseases

Prevention is better than cure. You can avoid trouble by growing resistant plants, maintaining clean conditions in the garden and greenhouse, and carrying out crop rotation on the vegetable plot.

• **Buy healthy plants** Seeds, plants, bulbs and other planting material should be obtained from reputable suppliers. Cheap lots from market stalls (or even the less reputable mail-order concerns) may be carrying pests and diseases that can take years to eliminate from a garden.

• **Buy resistant varieties** Choose varieties that are resistant or have a degree of tolerance to specific pests and diseases.

• **Rotation** As far as possible, avoid growing the same, or closely related, plants on one site in successive years, or soil-borne pests and diseases may build up. This applies as much to ornamental bedding plants as to vegetables. See p36.

• **Hygiene** Plants that have been badly attacked by pests and diseases should be removed and burnt. Do not leave rubbish lying around. Do not allow weeds to establish. Keep the greenhouse scrupulously clean.

• **Cultural control** The most important means of combating pests and diseases is by good cultural practice – for example, thorough soil preparations, feeding, watering, mulching, and correct methods of sowing and planting.

• **Biological control** The use of natural enemies to reduce the numbers of certain pests. At present this is used in a regulated way only in the greenhouse: the predatory mite *Phytoseiulus persimilis* for glasshouse red spider mite, and a parasitic wasp, *Encarsia formosa*, for glasshouse whitefly; all available from specialist producers. Don't forget the value of ladybirds, lacewings and wasps in the garden: they help to stamp out aphids (greenfly) and caterpillars.

■ Five ways to apply pesticides

There are several ways to apply pesticides (insecticides and fungicides), but whichever method you use you must follow the manufacturers' instructions. Otherwise plants may be damaged or pests and diseases inadequately controlled. With many pesticides there is a choice of methods.

• **Spraying** The most popular and usually the most effective and economical way of applying a chemical. The chemicals are sold in liquid concentrates or wettable powders which are mixed with water. Use a garden pressure sprayer with an adjustable nozzle. Various sizes are available. Spray in the evening when bees are back in hive. Do not spray when windy or when rain threatens.

• **Aerosols** Comparatively expensive but they require no mixing and are convenient for treating small numbers of plants. Especially useful for use in a greenhouse. Spray from the recommended distance.

• **Dusts** Also require no mixing. Useful for treating low-growing plants and those under attack by soil-borne pests and diseases. Less effective than sprays where it is necessary to have a good deposit of chemical on the undersides of leaves.

• **Granules** Some insecticides are formulated as granules which slowly release the chemical into the soil and so remain active against soil pests for a longer period than if the same chemical were applied as a spray or dust.

• **Smoke formulations** Smoke cones and canisters are available for treating certain greenhouse pests and diseases. You close down the greenhouse, light them and let the smoke and fumes kill off the pests and diseases overnight.

■ Two methods of action

There are two different ways in which chemicals work to control pests and diseases. Most fungicides act as protectants, in that they reduce infections by preventing the germination of fungus spores; hence it is important that you apply them before any symptoms are seen or at the very first signs of trouble.

• **Contact action** Most insecticides and some fungicides have this action. The pest or fungus is killed only when the chemical you apply comes directly into contact with it. You must therefore apply the chemical as thoroughly as possible on both sides of the foliage.

• **Systemic action** Some chemicals are systemic: that is, they are absorbed into the plant's tissues and move in the sap stream to parts that have not been sprayed directly. Systemic insecticides are particularly effective against sap-feeding pests, such as aphids. They are less effective against pests with chewing mouthparts, such as caterpillars: these are better controlled by contact insecticides. Systemic fungicides, such as benomyl and thiophanate-methyl, are not truly systemic since they are only translocated short distances inside the plants, and thus you have to use these types almost as frequently as any other types of fungicides.

■ Six watchpoints when applying pesticides

Work methodically, and pay due regard to safety: pesticides are potentially dangerous chemicals.

• **Follow manufacturer's instructions** Garden chemicals must be treated with respect at all times. Incorrect use may harm the user, as well as damage plants.

• **Protective clothing** When mixing and using chemicals it is advisable to wear rubber gloves. Wearing goggles will prevent splashes in the eyes.

• **Weather conditions** Avoid spraying or dusting in windy weather, as the chemicals may drift in the wind. The best conditions for spraying are when it is dry, calm and frost free.

• **Good coverage** Apply the spray evenly from all sides of the plant (always well away from you). Don't forget to spray the undersides of leaves.

• **Flowers** Generally, you should not use chemicals on plants that are in flower because this will endanger bees. In some cases, especially with fruit, spraying during flowering periods is recommended; but this must only be carried out at dusk when bees have returned to their hives.

• **Clean equipment** After spraying, thoroughly wash out the sprayer before storing it. Also wash protective clothing.

FLOWERING PLANTS

Most flowering plants are not much at risk as long as they are well cultivated. Among the principal sufferers are bulbs, and plants grown under glass, where pests and diseases particularly flourish.

■ Five troubles affecting roots

A number of insect pests live in the soil and feed on the roots of plants. Usually you do not know they're there until leaves and shoots begin to wilt.

• **Chafer grub** Long fat creamy-white grubs with brown heads which feed on the roots of many flowers. If suspected, water the soil with pirimiphos-methyl or dust with gamma-BHC.

• **Cutworm** Soil-dwelling caterpillars about 4cm/1½in long, creamy brown, which feed on roots and the surface of stems at soil level. Many border plants liable to attack. Symptom: wilting. Dust soil with gamma-BHC insecticide.

• **Millepede** Long thin insects with many legs, often black, curl up when disturbed. Often attack seedlings. Dust seedlings and soil with gamma-BHC insecticide.

• **Vine weevil** Grubs, about 1cm/½in long, white, with light brown heads, feed on roots, bulbs and tubers. Symptom: wilting. Dust soil with gamma-BHC insecticide.

• **Wireworm** Grubs of click beetles, up to 2.5cm/1in long, thin and wiry, orange-brown. They are often troublesome in new gardens where soil has been left undisturbed, eating roots of many plants, as well as bulbs, tubers and corms. Treat soil at planting time with bromophos insecticide.

■ Two troubles affecting bulbs and corms

Bulbous plants are subject to attack from the vine weevil and wireworm, as listed above. Here are two more serious troubles to watch out for:

• **Narcissus fly** Cream maggots feed inside narcissus or daffodil bulbs. They can kill the plants. Dust the soil and dying foliage of the bulbs with gamma-BHC dust at fortnightly intervals from mid-spring to early summer.

• **Rots** Various rots can affect bulbs, corms and tubers, especially when in storage. Store only when completely dry. Dip in benomyl fungicide beforehand. Regularly check stored material and discard bulbous plants that are starting to rot.

■ Five pests which make holes in leaves

Several serious pests feed on the leaves of a wide range of flowers, nibbling holes of various shapes and sizes.

• **Capsid bug** Usually green bugs, often found on chrysanthemums, dahlias and other plants. Masses of tiny holes in leaves. Apply dimethoate, gamma-BHC or fenitrothion insecticides.

• **Caterpillars** These may be green or brown. Small numbers can be picked off; otherwise apply gamma-BHC, fenitrothion or rotenone insecticides.

• **Flea beetle** Tiny blackish beetles creating a shot-hole effect in the leaves of many flowering plants especially wallflowers and aubrieta. Dust the affected plants with gamma-BHC, rotenone insecticides.

• **Slugs and snails** Will eat virtually any soft plant material: seedlings and young plants are particularly prone. Sprinkle slug pellets (based on metaldehyde) thinly around plants. Repeat if necessary.

• **Woodlice** Greyish "armour-plated" pests which go especially for seedlings and young plants. They feed at night and hide during the day. Metaldehyde slug pellets give some control; or dust seedlings with gamma-BHC.

■ Thirteen problems affecting leaves and stems

These are major pests and diseases, which can cripple the leaves and/or stems of ornamental flowering plants if not kept in check.

• **Aphids** Greenfly, blackfly and their relatives – an all too common sight in spring and summer. They cluster around shoot tips and their feeding causes stunted and distorted growth. They can cause the spread of disease. Very wide range of plants attacked. Colonies build up very quickly if not treated early. Spray with pirimicarb, malathion or rotenone.

• **Froghopper** Creamy-white bugs found on stems, covered with white froth, often known as 'Cuckoo spit'. Found in early summer. Either pick off by hand or spray plants with dimethoate or permethrin insecticides.

• **Grey mould** Common fungal disease affecting both outdoor and greenhouse plants. Causes rotting. Particularly prevalent in damp weather. Cut off affected parts and spray with benomyl or carbendazim fungicide.

• **Leafhopper** Greenish plant bugs, whose feeding habits result in pale mottling on leaves. Dust the affected plants with gamma-BHC insecticide.

• **Leaf miner** Small grubs which tunnel inside the leaves of plants such as chrysanthemums and delphiniums, producing silvery lines or blotches. Spray with Gamma-BHC, pirimiphos-methyl or pyrethrins insecticides.

• **Leaf spot** Many diseases cause brown or blackish spots on leaves of flowering plants. If not too many leaves are affected, pick them off; otherwise spray with a copper fungicide.

• **Mealy bug** Grey-white soft-bodied insects, covered with white silky wool, which feed on the stems of many greenhouse plants, such as cacti and succulents and shrubs. Spray regularly with malathion; or if plants are sensitive to this, dab the pests with methylated spirits.

• **Powdery mildew** Appears as a white powdery deposit on leaves and shoot tips of many plants. Severe attack can cause distortion. Often seen on chrysanthemums, Michaelmas daisies and delphiniums. Spray with benomyl or a sulphur fungicide.

• **Rust** Appears as rust-coloured pustules on the undersides of leaves of plants such as carnations, chrysanthemums, hollyhocks and antirrhinums. Destroy the affected leaves. Spray plants with mancozeb fungicide.

• **Scale** Scale-like brownish immobile insects found clustered on stems of greenhouse plants (sometimes also found outdoors). Spray with malathion.

• **Red spider mites** Microscopic red spider-like creatures whose feeding habits result in fine pale mottling on leaves of greenhouse plants. Spray regularly with malathion or dimethoate or pirimiphos-methyl. Or use biological control: the predatory mite *Phytoseiulus persimilis*.

• **Viruses** Classed as diseases. There are dozens of kinds, causing stunted or deformed growth and/or mottled or streaked foliage. There is no cure: affected plants should be dug up and burnt. Aphids spread viruses, so keep these under control.

• **Whitefly** A tiny white fly, found in colonies on the undersides of leaves of many plants under glass. Spray with pirimiphos-methyl, or fumigate the greenhouse with piri-mophos-methyl smoke. Or use biological control: the parasitic wasp *Encarsia formosa*.

■ Four troubles affecting flowers

Pests and diseases can attack the flowers of various ornamental plants, ruining the display unless they are dealt with in time.

• **Capsid bug** Often found on dahlias and chrysanthemums. They may kill flower buds, or cause the flowers to be deformed. See p150.

• **Earwig** Brown beetle-like creatures with rear pincers. They eat petals of chrysanthemums and dahlias. Spray with gamma-BHC or cypermethrin insecticides. Alternatively, trap by placing rolls of corrugated cardboard or clay pots loosely stuffed with straw among the plants. The earwigs hide there during the day and may be picked out and destroyed.

• **Grey mould** See p145.

• **Thrips** Tiny flies whose feeding habits result in silvery flecking on flowers. Gladioli particularly susceptible. Spray with dimethoate.

SHRUBS AND TREES
Many shrubs and trees are not much troubled by pests and diseases, although there are a few to watch out for. Roses have the most problems, especially the bush roses.

■ Four pests which make holes in leaves

These pests feed on the leaves, causing holes of various shapes and sizes. Caterpillars are the ones that usually cause most trouble.

• **Caterpillars** Caterpillars of various moths can cause a lot of damage to trees and shrubs – almost defoliating them in severe attacks. As soon as you see them, pick off by hand. In severe cases spray with fenitrothion, gamma-BHC or pirimiphos-methyl insecticides. The biological control *Bacillus thuringiensis* is also useful.

• **Chafer beetle** Cockchafer (3cm/1¼in long) and garden chafer (1.25cm/½in long), both brown, take out large holes in edges of leaves of many trees and shrubs in early summer. Most chafers also feed on flowers and fruits. If damage is severe spray with gamma-BHC insecticide.

• **Tortrix moth** The green or brown caterpillars of this moth spin leaves together and feed within, usually during early summer. Spray with fenitrothion.

• **Vine weevil** Adult is a long-snouted black beetle-like creature which eats notches out of edges of leaves of plants such as rhododendrons, azaleas and camellias. As soon as you notice damage, treat soil with the beneficial nematodes *Heterorhabditis megidis* or *Steinernema carpocapsae.*

■ Nine problems affecting leaves and shoots

These are all serious trouble-makers. They include the major rose diseases. Treat as soon as signs are seen and do not let any of them get out of hand.

• **Aphids** Greenfly, blackfly and other aphids attack many shrubs and trees. They cluster around shoot tips and their feeding causes stunted and distorted growth. As soon as you notice them, spray with pirimicarb, dimethoate, hepltenophos or pirimiphos-methyl insecticides.

• **Chlorosis** A physiological disorder. When lime or chalk in the soil prevents plants from absorbing iron, the leaves turn yellow. Chlorosis will occur if you plant lime-hating plants (eg rhododendrons and azaleas) in chalky or limy soil. It can also occur with roses or hydrangeas grown on very chalky soils; in which case, drench the soil around the plants with iron sequestrene. Grow lime-haters only in acid or lime-free soil.

• **Leaf miner** Small grubs feed inside leaves of plants such as holly, privet and lilac, making either silver channels or blister-like mines. Pick off affected leaves or spray with pirimiphos-methyl or pyrethrins.

• **Leaf spot** Collective term for several different fungal diseases which create brown or blackish spots on leaves. Many shrubs and trees are vulnerable. Spray with a copper fungicide as soon as you notice the problem.

• **Powdery mildew** Appears as a white powdery deposit on leaves and shoot tips of shrubs, including spindle bushes, mahonias and clematis. Severe attacks cause distortion. Spray with benomyl fungicide or sulphur.

• **Red spider mites** Several species of these microscopic spider-like creatures feed on leaves, causing a bronzy discoloration. Prevalent in hot dry weather. As soon as you see the symptoms, spray with malathion or dimethoate.

• **Rose black spot** The most common disease of roses. Circular dark brown or black spots, up to 1.25cm/1½in in diameter, develop on the leaves. In severe cases defoliation can occur. Spray fortnightly during growing season with myclobutanil or benomyl.

• **Rose mildew** Fungal disease causing a white floury coating on leaves, shoots and buds. Keep plants well watered, and spray regularly with benomyl or myclobutanil.

• **Rose rust** Fungal disease appearing as orange powdery pustules on undersides of leaves. The leaves fall prematurely. Spray with myclobutanil fungicide.

■ Four problems affecting roots and bark

Some of the following are serious and, if not dealt with early, can kill even large specimens

• **Canker** Several different fungi and bacteria cause canker, which appears as sunken and cracked areas in the bark. Sometimes wood underneath is exposed. A branch encircled by a canker will die. Cut out cankers back to healthy wood and paint wound with a proprietary tree paint.

• **Coral spot** Fungus, appearing as bright pink pustules on dead wood and twigs. Can spread to healthy wood, so cut out any dead stuff and paint wounds with a proprietary tree paint.

• **Honey fungus** Lethal fungal disease which can kill large trees. Kills roots and works its way up trunk, under the bark. First signs of attack are when branches or stems start dying, or fail to come into leaf in spring. In the autumn honey-coloured toadstools may appear round base of trunk or stems. A huge range of trees and shrubs are susceptible. If you start treatment soon enough you may be able to save an ailing specimen. Drench soil around plant with a proprietary formulation based on phenols, such as Armillatox.

• **Scale** Scale insects are immobile scale-like creatures found on stems and branches. May be brown, greyish or whitish. If only a few are present remove them by hand; otherwise spray plants with dimethoate, fatty acids or pyreturins.

LAWNS

The most common problem with lawns is discoloured turf. Mainly this is caused by some adverse cultural condition such as drought, waterlogging, faulty feeding or poor mowing. However, there are pests and diseases that can disfigure, weaken or even kill large areas of turf, so you should always investigate discoloured areas early and apply control measures, if needed, as soon as possible.

■ Three pests found in lawns

These are the most common, and most troublesome, pests that are likely to invade your lawn.

• **Earthworms** These expel small heaps of soil (wormcasts) on to the lawn surface. Wormcasts can make the lawn slippery and, if flattened by trampling or mowing, create muddy or bare patches which may be colonized by weeds. Worm activity is greatest in spring and autumn, when control measures should be undertaken. Water the lawn with carbaryl. Don't cut the lawn for one week after treatment.

• **Leatherjackets** The grubs of crane-flies (daddy-long-legs): 4cm/1½in long grey-brown maggots which feed on grass roots, causing yellow-brown patches during dry spells in summer. To detect, thoroughly water damaged areas and cover overnight with sacking or black polythene. Next day, any pests will be found lying on surface. Control by spraying lawn with pirimiphos-methyl, early autumn or early spring.

• **Moles** Their tunnelling can cause subsidence and uproot plants, and mole hills are unsightly and a general nuisance. Moles are difficult to control. Either place mole traps in the tunnels near mole hills, or control with mole smokes. Humane, ultra-sonic 'scare' devices are also available.

■ Three diseases of lawns

These are the most common and serious lawn diseases. They cause unsightly patches in the turf.

• **Fairy rings** Symptoms are lush green rings of grass between which, or in the middle of which, is brown dead grass or bare soil. Slender brown toadstools appear in summer and autumn. Make a number of holes in the brown area, squirt in washing-up liquid, and apply plenty of water. This should improve water penetration, but for a serious problem, it may be necessary to call in a contractor.

• **Red thread** Also known as corticium disease. Affects fine turf, usually in late summer or autumn. Pink patches appear but usually the grass is not killed. Red thread mostly develops where turf is poorly aerated and soil lacking in nitrogen. Rectify these faults. At first sign of trouble apply a fungicide or lawn dressing containing benomyl, carbendazim or dichlorophen.

• **Snow mould** Also known as fusarium patch. Can occur any time of year but most severe in mid-autumn, winter and spring. First shows as small patches of yellow dying grass, which later turn brown, increase in size and coalesce. The disease is encouraged by lack of aeration and excessive use of nitrogenous fertilizers. Rectify these faults. Water lawn with a fungicide containing benomyl, carbendazim or dichlorophen.

FRUITS

Fruits are especially prone to pests and diseases. The troubles dealt with here are those that reduce yields, damage the fruits or interfere with growth. Always buy plants certified to be healthy – in particular, free from viruses. Virused plants should always be dug up and burnt, as there is no cure.

■ Five troubles which result in holes in leaves

Some pests can cause serious damage to leaves and can strip a plant of foliage if not controlled.

• **Capsid bug** Pale green sap-sucking insect. Attacks shoot tips and young leaves of tree and bush fruits, leaving ragged holes. Spray the affected plants with systemic insecticide, such as dimethoate, after flowering or permethrin or pirimiphos-methyl just prior to flowering.

• **Caterpillars** The larvae of various moths can attack leaves of fruit trees, making many small holes. To control place grease bands around trunk of trees between mid-autumn and mid-spring to trap adult insects emerging from the soil; give the trees a tar-oil winter wash; spray against caterpillars with fenitrothion, bifenthurin or pyrethrins insecticides.

• **Gooseberry sawfly** Pale green caterpillars feed on leaves of gooseberries and currants. They can completely defoliate bushes. Spray with malathion, fenitrothion or rotenone insecticides.

• **Shot hole disease** Fungus which may attack cherry, peach, nectarine and plum trees if they are lacking in vigour. First brown spots appear, then small holes. Prevent by feeding, mulching and watering. Also spray the affected plants with copper fungicide in summer.

• **Tortrix moth** The caterpillars of this moth spin together leaves of tree fruits. Pick off or spray with fenitrothion, bifenthurin or fatty acid insecticides.

■ Eight problems affecting leaves and shoots

When pests and diseases cripple foliage or young shoots, the effect on the plants is debilitating.

• **Aphids** Greenfly, blackfly and other aphids attack all kinds of fruit trees and bushes. Give plants a tar-oil winter wash, and spray in spring/summer with a systemic insecticide such as pirimicarb or with fatty acids.

• **Cane spot** Disease which attacks raspberries, loganberries and hybrid berries. Shows as very small purple spots on leaves and on canes or stems. Spray with benomyl or carbendazim in spring and early summer.

• **Mildew** Appears as white powdery patches on leaves and shoot tips of both tree and bush fruits. As soon as you notice it, spray with benomyl or mancozet.

• **Peach leaf curl** Affects only peaches, nectarines, almonds and occasionally apricots. All or part of leaf becomes thickened and curled, bright red blisters develop. Where only a few leaves are affected, pick them off. Spray with mancozeb during mid- or late winter.

• **Red spider mite** Microscopic spider-like creatures which feed on the leaves of mainly tree fruits but also bush fruits. Results in pale yellow mottling. In late winter spray dormant plants with a wash containing tar oil; during spring and summer spray with malathion or a systemic insecticide.

• **Scab** Apple and pear scab are diseases which show as olive-green or brown blotches on leaves, which fall prematurely. Spray affected plants with benomyl, carbendazim or mancozeb in spring and summer.

• **Silver leaf** This fungal disease attacks mainly plums. The leaves turn silvery. Branches die back. Cut back all dead branches in summer to about 15cm/6in beyond where internal purple staining ceases. Paint wounds with tree paint. If tree is too badly affected, dig up and burn.

• **Woolly aphid** Grey-brown bug that is covered with white fluffy wax fibres. Occurs on stems of apples, causing the bark to develop soft lumpy galls. Spray with a systemic insecticide such as dimethoate.

■ Two problems affecting roots and bark

Several tree fruits are affected by cankers. These are serious diseases, and must be controlled.

• **Bacterial canker** The most serious disease of plums, can also be troublesome on peaches and cherries. Shows on branches as elongated flattened lesions from which exude copious amounts of gum. The branches die back. Remove cankered branches and dead wood and paint the wounds with tree paint. Spray foliage with a copper fungicide in summer and autumn.

• **Canker on apples and pears** Sunken and discoloured patches develop on the bark, which shrinks. The branch usually becomes swollen around the canker. If the branch becomes completely girdled it will die back. Cut out cankered branches. If there is no die-back, cut out cankers to healthy tissue. Paint all wounds with tree paint.

■ Three problems affecting buds and flowers

Birds usually create the biggest problem, but you should look out too for mites and weevils.

• **Apple blossom weevil** The small white grubs of this tiny brown beetle eat the central parts of apple flowers. Infested blossoms fail to open. Spray with permethrin as the buds are forming or fenitrothion as the buds burst open.

• **Big bud mites** Tiny mites that live in large numbers inside the buds of blackcurrants. Infected buds are swollen and round, and usually fail to come into growth. Pick off and burn; spray with benomyl fungicide in spring and early summer.

• **Birds** Bullfinches eat the unopened flower buds of cherries, plums, pears, apples, gooseberries and blackcurrants, usually attacking in small 'gangs' and causing severe damage very quickly. Protect plants by growing fruits in a fruit cage, or try deterrent sprays based on aluminium ammonium sulphate but these must be renewed after rain.

■ Eight problems affecting fruits

An assortment of pests, and one or two diseases, can ruin fruits before they are picked.

• **Apple sawfly** Maggots tunnel into young fruits, which fall prematurely. Protect fruits by spraying with dimethoate, permethrin or fenitrothion within 7 days of 80% petal fall.

• **Birds** Birds feed on the ripe fruits of most tree and bush fruits. Where possible, grow fruits in fruit cages; individual fruit trusses can be enclosed in bags made of muslin or old nylon tights.

• **Codling moth** The caterpillars of this moth tunnel into the maturing fruits of apples and pears. Protect by spraying the trees with fenitrothion in early summer with a second treatment 3 weeks later.

• **Grey mould** Can cause serious losses of strawberries, raspberries, currants, blackberries and other soft fruits during a wet summer. It shows as a greyish fluffy growth covering the fruits. Prevent infection by spraying with benomyl, carbendazim or sulphur just after flowering and repeat the treatment 3 times at fortnightly intervals.

• **Raspberry beetle** Pale brown grubs feed inside the ripening fruits of raspberries, blackberries and loganberries. Protect by spraying with rotenone bifenthrin or malathion: for raspberries when the first pink fruit develops, for loganberries at 80 per cent petal fall and again 2 weeks later, and for blackberries spray when the first flowers open. Spray at dusk when bees have returned to their hives.

• **Scab** Apple and pear scab produces brown or black scabs on the fruits. Spray infected trees with benomyl, carbendazim or mancozeb at bud burst, repeating the treatment every 2 weeks until late summer.

• **Slugs and snails** Most troublesome with strawberries: they eat the ripening fruits. Scatter slug pellets, based on methiocarb, thinly around the plants before damage occurs.

• **Wasps** Feed on most ripe tree fruits. The problem is that most wasps are also great friends of the gardener, as they attack caterpillars. To prevent attack, pick fruits as soon as they are ripe and before wasps take an interest. Allow fruits to ripen indoors if necessary.

VEGETABLES

Vegetables have to contend with numerous pests and diseases, but there are nowhere near as many problems today as in the past. This is partly due to treatments carried out by seed merchants before the sale of seeds or tubers, and partly to government restrictions on the varieties that can be sold. Some varieties of vegetables are now resistant, or partly resistant, to diseases. Crop rotation is an effective safeguard (see p36). Maintain hygienic conditions at all times. For example, eradicate weeds, as these can act as hosts for some pests and diseases, which can then spread to vegetables; do not leave rubbish (eg dead leaves or old plants) lying around.

■ Twelve problems affecting roots

C rop rotation will help to prevent a build-up of the serious troubles listed here.

• **Cabbage root fly** Maggots eat fine roots of cabbages and relations, until all that remains of root system is a blackened rotting stump. Wilting occurs. Treat soil with chlorpyrifos/daizinon or pirimiphos-methyl when sowing and planting.

• **Carrot fly** Maggots tunnel in the roots of carrots and parsnips. Treat seed drills with chlorpyrifos/diazinon or pirimiphos-methyl; carrots should be lifted as soon as they are ready to avoid damage from maggots.

• **Caterpillars** Chief culprits are those that feed on brassicas: the large and small cabbage white butterflies and the cabbage moth. Pick off small numbers by hand; alternatively, apply a chlorpyritos/diazinon soil insecticide close to the stems, or spray the plants with fenitrothion.

• **Clubroot** Disease that results in swollen distorted roots and severely stunted top growth. Affects all brassicas. Usually more troublesome in acid or lime-free soil. Apply lime if the soil is acid. Treat seedlings before planting by dipping roots in benomyl or a solution of thiophanate-methyl.

• **Cutworms** Soil-dwelling caterpillars of certain moths. They feed on roots, especially of lettuces, but of other vegetables also. The damaged plants wilt. Treat soil with a diazinon-based insecticide before sowing.

• **Onion fly** Maggots tunnel into the base of the bulbs and allow rots to enter. Treat the soil with a diazinon-based insecticide when sowing or planting.

• **Onion white rot** Fungal disease, showing as a white fluffy growth on roots and at base of bulb. Yellowing and subsequent death of leaves occur. Dig up and burn all affected onions.

153

Dust seed drills with benomyl and spray plants with a solution of benomyl.

• **Parsnip canker** Shows as rotting of the shoulder tissues of parsnips in autumn/winter. Grow resistant varieties such as 'Avonresister', and carry out crop rotation.

• **Potato blight** The most serious disease of potatoes. Yellow-brown patches occur on the leaves, which eventually turn brown or black. A reddish-brown dry rot affects the tubers. Spray maincrop potatoes in mid-summer with a copper fungicide or treat with mancozeb. Grow resistant varieties such as 'Maris Peer'.

• **Potato scab** Causes superficial raised scabs with ragged edges on potato tubers. Common in dry, sandy or gravelly soils. Improve humus content. Liming encourages the disease. Grow resistant varieties such as 'Arran Pilot', 'Maris Peer'.

• **Slugs** Small black soil-dwelling slugs make holes in tubers of potatoes and roots of other vegetables. Metaldehyde (see p61 BAA) slug pellets will help reduce the slug population. Avoid organic fertilizers where there is a slug problem. Harvest potatoes as soon as possible rather than leaving them in the ground to be eaten. Another method is to set slug traps, which you sink into the soil and fill with stale beer.

• **Wireworm.** The larvae of click beetles: thin, wiry, orange. Mainly a problem in new gardens, feeding on tubers of potatoes and roots of other vegetables. Treat soil with chlorpyrifos/diazinon or pirimiphos-methyl at sowing or planting time.

■ Eight troubles affecting stems and leaves

A varied assortment of both pests and diseases can harm stems and leaves of vegetable crops.

• **Aphids** Greenfly and blackfly congregate on shoot tips of such vegetables as broad beans, runner beans, potatoes and peas. Spray with a specific aphicide such as pirimicarb.

• **Birds** Wood pigeons peck destructively at foliage of brassicas, especially in winter. Grow in a netting cage.

• **Downy mildew** White fungal disease found on leaves of lettuces, onions, spinach and young brassicas. At first signs of trouble, remove affected leaves and spray with mancozeb.

• **Flea beetles** Tiny beetles which eat holes in leaves of brassica seedlings. Control with rotenone, gamma-BHC seed dressing or pirimiphos-methyl.

• **Glasshouse red spider mite** Common greenhouse pest, causing fine pale mottling on leaves, which adversely affects growth. Keep atmosphere moist. Spray with bifenthrin or fatty acids at 7-day intervals; or use biological control.

• **Glasshouse whitefly** Tiny white fly, another serious pest of crops grown under glass. Spray with fatty acids, pyrethrins or dimethoate methyl at 7-day intervals, or use biological control.

• **Powdery mildew** Leaves and stems of several vegetables become covered with a white powdery coating. Control the disease by spraying with benomyl sulphur or carbendazim, repeating as necessary.

• **Slugs and snails** Attack many vegetables, particularly seedlings. Sprinkle slug pellets, based on metaldehyde, thinly around plants before trouble starts.

∎ Three troubles affecting fruits and pods

D o not let fruits, such as tomatoes, succumb to rots, nor peas to attacks by insects.

• **Greymould** This a fungal disease, showing as a grey fluffy mould. Most prevalent in wet summers, it can cause rotting of tomatoes, marrows and other fruits, and pod. As soon as you notice it, pick off affected fruits and spray affected plants with benomyl fungicide.

• **Pea moth** The caterpillars feed on the developing seeds inside pods. Peas which come into flower between early summer and late summer should be sprayed with fenitrothion (at dusk) 7 days after the start of flowering.

• **Pea thrips** Tiny black insects which feed on pods and foliage of peas. Shows as a silvery-brown discolouration on the pods, which may be malformed and contain only a few peas. Worse in hot dry summers. Spray with fenitrothion or malathion as soon as noticed.

GLOSSARY

Numbers in brackets refer to pages on which the term is more fully explained.

Acid Describes soil with a pH of below 7.

Aeration The process of spiking a lawn in order to allow air into the soil and relieve compaction. (135)

Alkaline Describes soil with a pH over 7.

Annual A plant that completes its life-cycle within one growing season. (65)

Bare-root plant A plant lifted from the open ground (as opposed to a container-grown plant). (51)

Bedding plant A plant used for temporary garden display. (51)

Biennial A plant that completes its life-cycle over two growing seasons. (65)

Brassica The cabbage, cauliflower and turnip genus of the Cruciferae.

Bulb An underground storage organ that consists of layers of swollen fleshy leaves or leaf bases, which enclose the following year's growth buds. (80)

Bush tree A tree pruned to give a dwarf form with about 60–75cm/2–2½ft of clear stem.

Cane fruits Fruiting plants that produce long cane-like stems, often prickly, such as raspberries and blackberries.

Canker A sharply defined diseased area on a woody stem, which often has malformed bark. (148, 151)

Climber A plant that climbs by clinging to objects by means of twining stems with hooks or tendrils, or more generally, any long-stemmed plant trained upwards. (90)

Compost, garden Rotted organic matter used as an addition to or substitute for manure. (37–8, 64)

Compost, seed and potting Mixtures of organic and inorganic materials, such as peat, sand and loam, used for growing seeds, cuttings and pot plants.

Conifer A plant that bears its seeds in cones.

Contact insecticide An insecticide that kills pests by direct contact. (142)

Cordon A normally branched tree or shrub restricted by spur pruning to a single-stem. (59)

Corm A solid, swollen stem-base, resembling a bulb, that acts as a storage organ. (80)

Cultivar See Variety.

Cutting A separated piece of stem, root, or leaf taken in order to propagate a new plant.

Dead-head To prune the spent flowers or the unripe seedpods from a plant. (57)

Division The technique of splitting clump-forming plants into a number of portions, complete with roots and buds/top growth. (43)

Dwarf pyramid A tree pruned to form a pyramid-shaped central-leader tree about 2m/7ft high.

Ericaceous A plant belonging to the Ericaceae family, which contains heathers, rhododendrons and azaleas. Most plants in this family are lime-haters and should be grown in acid soil.

Espalier A tree trained with a vertical main stem and tiers of horizontal branches. (60)

Family A group of related genera. For example, the genera *Poa* (meadow grass), *Festuca* (fescue) and *Agrostis* (bent) all belong to the family of grasses, Graminea.

Fan A shrub or tree in which the main branches are trained like the ribs of a fan against a wall, fence or other support system. (60)

Fertile soil (rich soil) A soil that is well-supplied with plant foods (provided by fertilizers) and with humus (provided by bulky organic matter).

Fertilizer Materials that provides plant food. It can be organic, i.e. derived from decayed plant or animal matter, or organic, i.e., made from chemicals. (33–4)

Genus (*plural genera*) A group of allied species in botanical classification.

Germination The development of a seed into a seedling.

Groundcover plant A plant that is capable, especially when planted in a group, of completely covering the soil with stems and foliage, effectively suppressing annual weeds. (117–20)

Half-hardy A plant unable to survive the winter unprotected but not needing all-year-round greenhouse protection. (65–6)

Half-standard A tree grown with 0.9–1.2m/3–4ft of clear stem. (60)

Harden off To acclimatize plants raised in warm conditions to colder conditions.

Hardy Describes a plant capable of surviving the winter in the open without protection. (65)

Herbaceous perennial *See* Perennial.

Hormone rooting powder A powder containing special chemicals which induces root formation in cuttings. (39)

Humus Fertile, organic matter that is in an advanced stage of decay.

Hybrid A plant produced by the cross fertilization of two species or variants of a species.

John Innes Compounds Standard soil mixes that can be easily reproduced to give good results. Developed at the John Innes Horticultural Institute in 1939. Revolutionized the growing of plants in pots. (64)

Layering Propagating by inducing shoots to form roots while they are still attached to the parent plant. (43–4)

Leader shoot The shoot that is dominating growth in a stem system, and is usually uppermost.

Leaf mould Well-rotted leaves, which can be used as a mulch or added to the soil to improve its texture.

Microclimate The climatic conditions in a particular small area. (5)

Mulch A top-dressing of organic or inorganic matter, applied to the soil around a plant. (39)

Pan A hard layer of soil beneath the surface.

Perennial A plant that lives for more than three seasons. (73)

pH The degree of acidity or alkalinity. Below 7 on the pH scale is acid, above it is alkaline.

Pinching (or stopping) The removal of the growing tip of a shoot.

Pricking out The transplanting and spacing out of seedlings. (42)

Propagation The production of a new plant from an existing one, either sexually by seeds or vegetatively, for example by cuttings. (39–50)

Rhizome A creeping horizontal underground stem that acts as a storage organ.

Rooting cutting A piece of the root of a plant used for propagation. (44–5)

Rootstock *See* Grafting.

Rose (spray head) The watering can or hose attachment producing a fine spray.

Runner A rooting stem that grows along the surface of the soil, as in strawberries.

Scarifying The process of vigorously raking a lawn in order to remove thatch. (134–5)

Self-sterile Describes a plant whose pollen cannot fertilize its own female parts.

Shrub A perennial plant with persistent woody stems branching from the base. If only the lower parts of the branches are woody and the upper shoots are soft and usually die in winter, it is known as a sub-shrub. (106)

Species A group of closely related organisms within a genus.

Spike A vertical stem bearing short-stalked flowers for all or part of its length. Some are very tall, as in delphiniums; others are short, as in grape hyacinths.

Spur A slow-growing short branch system that usually carries clusters of flower beds.

Standard A tree or shrub grown with 1.5–2m/5–7ft of clear stem.

Sub-soil *See* Top-soil.

Sub-species A category intermediate between a variety and a species.

Sucker A shoot growing from a stem or root at or below ground level.

Systemic fungicide or insecticide A chemical which permeates a plant's sap stream and kills biting or sucking insects. (142)

Tap root The primary vertical root of a plant; also any strong-growing vertical root.

Thin To reduce the number of seedlings, beds, flowers, fruitlets or branches. (41)

Top-dressing *See* Dressing.

Top-soil The upper layer of dark fertile soil in which plants grow. Below this lies the sub-soil, which is lighter in colour, lacks organic matter and is often low in nutrients.

Tuber A swollen underground stem or root that acts as a storage organ and from which new plants or tubers may develop. (80–1)

Variety A distinct variant of a species; it may be a cultivated form (a cultivar) or occur naturally (varietas).

Wall shrub A shrub grown against a wall or fence. It is not necessarily trained flat, although some shrubs can be so trained if desired; neither is it a true climber. (90)

INDEX OF PLANT NAMES